THINGS TO DO IN HOT SPRINGS BEFORE YOU DIE

Fountain
WAX

100 THINGS TO DO IN HOT SPRINGS BEFORE YOU DIE

CASSIDY KENDALL

Reedy Press
PO Box 5131
St. Louis, MO 63139, USA
www.reedypress.com

Library of Congress Control Number: 2021950827

ISBN: 9781681063485

Design by Jill Halpin

Cover photo courtesy of Visit Hot Springs. All other photos by the author unless otherwise noted.

Printed in the United States of America
22 23 24 25 26 5 4 3 2 1

DEDICATION

For my sweet grandparents,
who introduced me to the magic of Hot Springs.

For my sisters, who made it a home.

For the community, who cherish Hot Springs's traditions and work tirelessly to keep it growing, making it a welcoming destination for all.

NATIONAL
PARK
SERVICE
Hot Springs
National Par
National Park Service
U.S. Department of the Interior

CONTENTS

Music and Entertainment

Sports and Recreation

Culture and History

Shopping and Fashion

PREFACE

Like many, I was first introduced to Hot Springs as a vacation destination. During my childhood in Southern Arkansas, my sweet grandparents would regularly whisk me and my two sisters away to enjoy a week of lake life during the summers. The excitement we felt seeing the sparkle of Lake Hamilton as we crossed the bridge coming in on 70 West after having travelled nearly two hours is just as vivid today as it was many years ago. We knew what these weeks brought: mist on our faces as we cruised the lake in our family's party barge; the joy found in a friendly game of putt-putt at Pirate's Cove; a beautiful drive up Hot Springs Mountain and into the Mountain Tower to see the breath-taking views; and a stroll through downtown to window shop and simply enjoy the days spent in the Spa City.

After childhood, I thought my magical summers in Hot Springs were over as I grew older and went out into the world. But as fate would have it, I was brought back here on a more permanent basis after I graduated college. I had the rare opportunity to be reintroduced to the most magical place I had ever been to. And while I still got to enjoy all the things I had before, like the lake, nature, and yes, still games of putt-putt at Pirate's Cove, I found there was a whole other world of beauty and magic to be experienced in Hot Springs year-round.

As a local newspaper journalist I quickly got acquainted with the community after moving here. I learned it's the locals that keep the town that magical destination I had remembered from so many years before. I discovered a laugh brought by the community theatre at a Pocket show, a profound thought incited by a Wednesday Night Poetry, the beauty found in a downtown Gallery Walk, the quirkiness of a World's Shortest St. Patrick's Day Parade, and the glamour of a documentary film festival having run longer than any other in North America. I also found a library that would go above and beyond to accommodate its community, more hiking trails and swimming holes than I could ever imagine, and a historic Bathhouse Row that still has some bathhouses for bathing—but also one that brews beer with the local "magical" thermal water, and another run by the city's Mayor offering a grand hotel and one of the best brunches you'll have in your life. I could go on and on, but the point is I got lucky enough to meet Hot Springs twice in my lifetime, and now I would like nothing more than to share the country's best-kept secret with the readers of this book.

Hot Springs is known as the Spa City for the millennia-old thermal waters deriving from the mountain that drew in people from all over the world for medicinal bathing and soaking. Tasting and bathing in these waters today are the obvious "must-do's" when finding yourself in Hot Springs, but whether you're visiting or living here, count yourself lucky and enjoy it for all it's worth.

In this book you will read 100 things I have deemed important enough to do while in Hot Springs before you die. I've lived in Hot Springs for three years, but have frequented it my entire life, so I hope to appeal to both the visitor and local in these pages, which will introduce you to some of the best foods, businesses, places, events, and historical tidbits in the area, as well as insider tips that will help you make the most of your time spent in one of the best places on earth.

FOOD AND DRINK

1

STEP INTO HISTORY
AND SAVOR AN OHIO CLUB BURGER

Once a hopping joint for the gangsters who frequented Hot Springs, the Ohio Club has been the oldest club in Arkansas since 1905. It's now loved by the masses and known for its history, live music and—just as importantly—its burgers. These award-winning, handcrafted burgers made with a special-blended meat mixed fresh daily and decorated with fresh local produce are *to die for*. They pair best with the spicy fried green beans and a Madden No. 1 (the Superior Bathhouse Brewery light ale paying homage to infamous gangster Owney Madden, who called Hot Springs home for 30 years). With a mix of great food and rich history, the Ohio Club is a prime place to start when getting to know Hot Springs better. Begin your journey by stepping into this historic site and dine among the lingering spirits of the gangsters.

336 Central Ave., 501-627-0702
theohioclub.com

2

STUFF YOUR BIG MOUTH
WITH THE BAILEY'S SPECIAL

Bailey's Dairy Treat has spent nearly 30 years perfecting its brown-paper-bag meals and milkshakes, and the Bailey's Big Mouth Special—complete with a cheeseburger, fries, and drink—gives you a taste of what this classic drive-in diner has to offer. Choose anything from burgers to egg rolls, pizza sticks, or chicken fried steak. And no matter what you get, top it off with one of Bailey's famous, creamy, delicious milkshakes. Don't blink or you may miss this tiny treasure located off Park Avenue. But if you know what you're looking for, the iconic flashing neon "Bailey's" sign atop the diner will call you home to this nostalgic classic eatery that has lived in the hearts of Hot Springians for decades.

510 Park Ave., 501-624-4085
facebook.com/burgersareyum

TIP

On the Bailey's Big Mouth Special, you can (and totally should) upcharge the drink for a shake.

3

BATHE IN THERMAL WATER BREW
AT SUPERIOR

Everything is unique about Superior Bathhouse Brewery. It's in a historic bathhouse, and its beer is brewed with Hot Springs's thermal waters. In this eclectic parlor you will find 18 distinctive beers brewed in-house, and for just $35 you can order the "beer bath," which allows you to try them all. In addition to beer, Superior also brews its own delicious root beer that is a must-try whether you're a root beer enthusiast or not, because how many people can you say they've delighted their palates with root beer brewed with 4,000-year-old *magical water*? And don't forget about the food when you go—talk about some of the freshest "pub grub" you'll ever come across.

329 Central Ave., 501-624-2337
superiorbathhouse.com

TIP

While Arkansas laws prohibit carry-out alcohol sales on Sunday (as of 2021), Superior has a special permit to sell growlers to-go, 7-days a week.

OTHER PLACES WITH A SUNDAY CARRY-OUT LOOPHOLE

SQZBX Brewery and Pizza Joint
236 Ouachita Ave., 501-609-0609
sqzbx.com

Bubba Brew's
1252 Airport Rd., 501-547-3186
bubbabrews.com

Crystal Ridge Distillery
455 Broadway St., 501-627-0722
crystalridgedistillery.com

The Winery
1503 Central Ave., 501-623-9463
hotspringswinery.com

Bathhouse Row Winery
220 Central Ave., 501-620-4880
hotspringswinery.com

HEAD TO WILL'S

FOR THE BEST CINNAMON ROLL OF YOUR LIFE

"The best cinnamon roll of your life" is a bold statement, but over the past few years Will's Cinnamon Shop has proved it can deliver. Everything made at the shop is made from scratch; no box mixes or shortcuts taken. Just a roll with multiple icings and toppings to choose from will give you your fix, but if you're visiting during the fall you *do not* want to miss out on the apple pie roll. It's just apple pie filling made with fresh apples on top of a cinnamon roll—simple, but insanely delicious, which is what Will's is best at. Once held in a dine-in restaurant, Will himself now only serves bulk orders of cinnamon rolls from the back of what has changed from Will's Cinnamon Shop to Destiny's Bakeshop. But don't worry, if you're still looking for a dine-in experience for just a single roll, Destiny's will be selling Will's products for him too.

1001 Central Ave., 501-538-4650
willscs.com

5

GO HOME
TO THE PANCAKE SHOP

Since 1940, The Pancake Shop in downtown Hot Springs has been delighting the masses with their true homemade breakfast. Here at one of the oldest family-owned and operated restaurants in the state, every guest is welcomed to the shop's table and served with a unique dining experience. The orange juice is freshly squeezed, the pancakes are made from scratch, the sausage is homemade, the ham is award-winning, and the whole experience shouldn't be missed. In fact, it's so popular that anyone going on a Saturday or Sunday should be sure to get there early and prepare to wait outside for a table to become available. But believe me, the wait to dine here is *well* worth it.

216 Central Ave., 501-624-5720
pancakeshop.com

PSSTT . . . ONE MORE PANCAKE SHOP TO TRY

Colonial Pancake & Waffle House
111 Central Ave., 501-624-9273

TIP

If you enjoyed your meal at The Pancake Shop, check out its next-door store, The Savory Pantry, to pick up more of the ham, sausage, apple butter, or coffee to enjoy again and again at home.

SQUEEZE IN

A SQZBX PIE AND BREW

In this retro musically themed pizza joint and brewery located in a restored historic building, pick up a hand-tossed New Jersey–style pie with a mug of beer brewed in-house. The pizza's crust is thin with dough made fresh daily, and the toppings are from only the freshest produce. The pie is then crisped to perfection in a rotating stone oven. And the beer—*oh, the beer*. It's made in-house by co-owner Zac Smith, and there are between four and six beers available at any given time. Look to The Perfecta American Light Ale and Hard Cider as menu staples that never disappoint. The Perfecta is everything you could want and more in a light ale, and the Hard Cider is, unlike most ciders, unpasteurized, resulting in a cloudy cider with a clean, dry flavor profile. But the safest bet may be to opt for a flight so you don't miss any of Smith's seasonal concoctions while dining at SQZBX.

236 Ouachita Ave., 501-609-0609
sqzbx.com

TIP

SQZBX is connected to KUHS, a community nonprofit radio that plays a little bit of everything at 102.5 FM.

SIX MORE MOUTH-WATERING PIZZA JOINTS

Rocky's Corner
2600 Central Ave., 501-624-0199

DeLuca's Pizzeria
831 Central Ave., 501-609-9002
delucas.pizza

Maxine's Live
700 Central Ave., 501-321-0909
maxineslive.com

Grateful Head
100 Exchange St., 501-781-3405
gratefulheadpizza.com

Beano's
2230 Malvern Ave., Ste. D, 501-262-3266
beanospizza.com

Sam's Pizza Pub
401 Burchwood Bay Rd., 501-525-0780
samspizzapub.net

7

SNAG A PRETZEL
FROM THE BIERGARTEN OF STEINHAUS KELLER

In the depths of Spencer's Corner in downtown Hot Springs you can find yourself in the Bavarian region of Germany. On its interior, Steinhaus Keller has dim lighting, exposed rock, and barrelled ceilings to create the atmosphere of a German ratskeller. On its exterior you will find a beautiful stone biergarten that—as long as the weather is dry—you should almost always opt for. But enough with the physicalities, let's explore the *delicacies* found on the menu. From schnitzel to gourmet charcuterie boards to giant, hanging Bavarian pretzels paired with haus-made bier cheese and spicy brown mustard, Steinhaus has a wide variety of authentic German foods to choose from. And speaking of variety, the restaurant also has the state's largest selection of German and European beer. What are you waiting for? An evening full of culture awaits.

801 Central Ave., Ste. 15, 501-624-7866
steinhauskeller.com

8

HAVE YOUR PICK
AT 420 EATS FOOD TRUCK COURT

420 Eats Food Truck Court caters to everyone's tastes in food and fun. This outdoor space just outside of downtown has games, live music events, a full bar, and up to six food trucks that have something for everyone, so no one leaves disappointed. It's even pet friendly, so when I say everyone, I mean no one gets left behind. Around the fenced-in court you will find games like baggo, ringo, Connect 4, ping pong, Jenga, and dominos. Artists and doodlers are also encouraged to bring markers and make their mark on the court's pavilion. Also, check the 420 Eats Food Truck Court Facebook Page before planning a night to go so you can catch an evening of live musical performances by both local and traveling artists.

420 Malvern Ave., 501-420-3286
facebook.com/420eats

TAKE A SIP FROM THE CREEK
AT CRYSTAL RIDGE DISTILLERY

We're talking moonshine, baby, and lots of it. Moonshine was a southern staple during the prohibition days, and making it (though not always legal) was arguably a necessary activity to feed families. Today, making *legal* moonshine has proved to be just as lucrative, and Hot Springs natives Danny and Mary Bradley have started the first legal moonshine distillery in Hot Springs. Moonshine flavors like apple pie, salted caramel, maple bacon, pecan pie, grape, peach, pineapple, and strawberry (just to name a few) have been produced from this down-home distillery, and the Bradley's are continuously creating new flavors. Enjoy your moonshine at the bar, have them mix it into a cocktail if you please, partake in a tasting, or grab a jar to take home. With their large variety of flavors, you're sure to find something that tickles your fancy.

455 Broadway St., 501-627-0722
crystalridgedistillery.com

SIP A BANANA PIÑA COLADA AT SUNSET

AT BUBBA BREWS

The view of Lake Hamilton from the patios of Bubba Brews Sports Pub and Grill is the cherry on top of a summer's day in the tri-lakes area. Some might even say it's the best spot in town to watch a sunset over the lake, and I might say the banana piña colada is the best drink to indulge in while doing so. But while the view makes for a perfect piña-colada moment, it isn't called Bubba *Brews* for nothing. I would be remiss not to mention their stellar selection of locally brewed beer—a fan-favorite being Bubba's Bloodhound Blood Orange, a refreshing pale ale perfect for the lake, brewed with over 80 pounds of blood oranges. So perhaps *after* that banana piña colada, take a gander at their beer menu. But above all else, enjoy yourself to the fullest; you're in the right place to do so.

1252 Airport Rd., 501-547-3186
bubbabrews.com

11

BRUNCH YOUR HEART OUT
AT EDEN

Eden, the luxurious restaurant located inside Hotel Hale on Bathhouse Row, has one of the largest weekend brunch offerings around. Take a seat under the glass ceiling of this beautiful historic structure that was once a bathhouse, and take your pick from all your favorite brunch contenders. Eden has the classics—eggs benedict, chicken and waffles, french toast, quiche or omelets—or perhaps try something new and opt for eggs sardou, shrimp and grits or the bacon and jam sandwich. And let's not forget about drinks! What's brunch without mimosas of the variety? Try a flight that serves six with six different juice options and five different champagne options, or get a single glass of one of Eden's specialty mimosas, like the Berry Good, Hibiscus, or Strawberry Pineapple. Venture to Eden; inside, there is a classy brunch awaiting you.

341 Central Ave., 501-760-9010
hotelhale.com

TIP

Reservations are recommended for weekend brunch, even if it's same-day reservations.

CAN'T GET INTO EDEN?
HERE ARE SEVEN BRUNCH ALTERNATIVES

Best Cafe
638 Ouachita Ave., 870-474-6350
facebook.com/bestcafeandbar

Argentinian
328 Central Ave., 501-623-2777
facebook.com/coffeewinebar

The Arlington
(Sunday only)
239 Central Ave., 501-623-7771
arlingtonhotel.com

The Avenue
340 Central Ave., 501-321-0001
theavenuehs.com

Kollective
110 Central Ave., 501-701-4000
kollectivecoffeetea.com

Java Primo
4429 Central Ave., Ste. A, 501-318-9789
Javaprimo.com

Track Kitchen
171 Golf Links Rd., 501-363-4775
oaklawn.com

12

BRING YOUR BOTTOM
TO FAT BOTTOMED GIRL'S

Award-winning cupcakes so good they grabbed the attention of the Food Network television series *Cupcake Wars* in 2013 can be found at Fat Bottomed Girl's Cupcake Shoppe. These giant, moist, delicious gourmet cupcakes have become a staple within the Hot Springs community. For first-timers, a good introduction to the confection perfection served here is the best-selling Ooey Gooey Buttercake, based on a traditional St. Louis–style butter cake. Other signature flavors include salted caramel, crème brûlée and lemon lavender. But this cupcakery is no place to play it safe. Dive into some of the more wild flavors they have been known to offer, like buttered popcorn, sour head or salted watermelon. The cupcakes are made fresh each morning, and they never disappoint.

502 Central Ave., 501-318-0997
fbgcupcakes.com

TIP

You can't miss the connected gift and ice cream shop when visiting Fat Bottomed Girls, but don't forget to venture up the street to Fat Bottomed Girls Puppy Bakery, located at 120 Central Avenue, to snag a sweet treat for your four-legged friend, too.

13

BUILD A UNIQUE PLATE
AT CAFÉ 1217

Looking for some of the freshest gourmet food around? Head to Café 1217 for a delicious experience. Pick from their glass encasement of freshly made yummies as your mouth waters to build a plate that will satisfy you. Their motto is "freshest and finest," and it's completely accurate at this café, where they use real and whole food, "relying on food's natural beauty & flavor to speak for itself." It's seasonal, creative, and healthy. At the café, they put good in to get good out, so you can fill your tummy guilt-free as you experience truly unique flavors. But be sure to save room for dessert! Just like the main entrées, the sweets are homemade too, and you simply can't pass up a homemade treat.

1217 Malvern Ave., 501-318-1094
cafe1217.net

COOL OFF
AT MAMOO'S CREAMERY

The only thing better than homemade ice cream is homemade ice cream served in a homemade waffle cone. Mamoo's Creamery makes everything in house and prides itself in creating unique, handcrafted creamy dairy treats to be enjoyed by anyone visiting downtown. When that sweet tooth strikes, you may want to give the shop's best seller, Southern Bourbon Butter Pecan, a taste. But among the 36 flavors offered they have had a few zany contenders come through that have been just as popular. Allow me to list just a few of the concoctions coming out of Mamoo's kitchen. We've got Revenge of the Nerds, a cotton candy ice cream with Nerds candies; Midnight Fire, a chocolate ice cream with a heated aftertaste; Captain Crunch Berries, paying homage to an unbeatable cold bowl of cereal; and Peanut Butter and Jelly, an ice cream strangely resembling the actual sandwich, including the bread. Mamoo's offers dairy-free flavors, and most of their offerings are naturally gluten-free. As a self-proclaimed ice cream connoisseur, I'm telling you: When in need, hit Mamoo's Cream.

239 Central Ave., Ste. E, 501-463-9488
mamoosparadice.com

FIVE OTHER PLACES TO SCREAM OVER

Kilwins
264 Central Ave., 501-701-4464
kilwins.com

Dolcé Gelato
222 Cornerstone Blvd., 501-525-6580
dolcegelato.co

Kringles and Kones
115 A Central Ave., 501-625-9903

Pour Some Sugar on Me
502 Central Ave., 501-701-4443
poursomesweets.com

King Kone
1505 Malvern Ave., 501-321-9766

15

TAKE YOUR SHOES OFF, HAVE A ROLL, AND STAY AWHILE

AT OSAKA

Indulge in one (or a few) of the authentic, freshly made sushi rolls at one of the private tatami tables at Osaka Japanese Steakhouse & Sushi Bar. This Hot Springs staple that mixes authentic Japanese culture and food with a classic and contemporary atmosphere can meet all your sushi and hibachi needs. Want a more lively dining experience? Take a seat at the hibachi grill and allow the chef to wow you as he prepares a fiery meal before his audience. But whether you opt for a roll, hibachi, or one of Osaka's other authentic creations, a word to the wise: Everything pairs well with their homemade miso soup and a bottle of their nigori sake.

3954 Central Ave., Ste. M, 501-525-9888
osakahotsprings.com

TWO OTHER SUSHI BARS WORTH YOUR TIME

Crazy Samurai
5431 Central Ave., 501-525-0488
facebook.com/
crazysamuraihotsprings

Ai Sushi and Grill
1609 Albert Pike Rd., Ste. J
501-701-4323
aisushihs.com

ENJOY A DRINK AND A VIEW

FROM THE ROOFTOP OF THE WATERS

The Rooftop Bar at The Waters Hotel provides one of the best views of historic downtown Hot Springs. This luxurious area atop one of the tallest historic buildings in the area is best enjoyed at night under the string lights and moonlight. Even in the wintertime the gusty high dining area is comfortable (with a jacket) near the numerous outdoor heaters provided. Go to the rooftop for a dinner or an after-dinner drink. Either way, incorporating it into a night out on downtown Hot Springs is a must. It's also a pretty popular spot, so calling ahead of time to make a reservation is never a bad idea. My recommendations are the Chicken Sammy paired with a gin and tonic. In the wintertime, try their signature holiday eggnog.

340 Central Ave., 501-321-0001
thewatershs.com

EAT GOURMET ON-THE-GO
AT BUBBALU'S

When you find yourself in downtown Hot Springs looking for fast, cheap food, yet made with some of the best and freshest ingredients, look to none other than BubbaLu's. This family-friendly, 1950s-style diner can be found nestled between downtown merchants; just look for the red and white striped awning. They serve up fresh-pressed burgers, classic hot dogs, chili, and copious amounts of onion rings and fries. And the beauty of BubbaLu's is that you can have that classic diner experience eating in, or you can have a hassle-free carryout basket in 10 minutes or less, meaning you won't have to break stride in your downtown browsing while you walk and devour. You can't beat the classics, and BubbaLu's has mastered them all.

408 Central Ave., 501-321-0101
facebook.com/bubbalus

18

TASTE THE FLAVOR BURST
AT KING KONE

Head to this classic drive-in diner to satisfy any ice cream hankering you may have. King Kone has some of the best soft-serve ice cream around (which are big words for a place that's close to a Sonic Drive-In, but trust me, it's really good.) They have all the classics, from banana splits to dip cones, but one concoction that you shouldn't pass up if you've never had it is their signature "flavor burst" cone. This swirl of flavored syrup and soft serve ice cream is a uniquely delicious option. My personal flavor burst recommendation is the refreshing and delectable orange and vanilla. But I should also mention there are a slew of other options besides sweets at King Cone, including a wide variety of burgers, hot dogs, chicken, and more.

1505 Malvern Ave., 501-321-9766

19

GET DIRTY WITH THE CHEESE
AT PICANTE'S

Located in downtown Hot Springs's Spencer's Corner, Picante's Mexican Grill is the place to go when you need your cheese dip fix, and in this case even your dirty cheese dip fix. Head to Picante's and ask for this nonmenu item that will blow your mind. It's a three layer dip that starts with a bean base, topped with tereso, topped with queso. Want to spice it up? Mix in a little of Picante's habanero salsa. You could have this as a meal on its own, or order it as an appetizer for the table and indulge in any one of Picante's other authentic Mexican dishes for your main course. But whatever you do, be sure to complete your dining experience with one of Picante's thirst-quenching margaritas!

801 Central Ave., Ste. 22, 501-623-2300
picantesmexicangrill.com

MORE MEXICAN

Quetzal
1105 Albert Pike Rd., 501-881-4049
orderquetzalar.com

La Bodeguita
1313 Central Ave., 501-620-4967
510 Albert Pike Rd., 501-609-9580

Jose's
2215 Malvern Ave., 501-609-9700
5361 Central Ave., 501-525-9797
josesmexicangrill.com

Taco Mama
1209 Malvern Ave., 501-624-6262
510 Ouachita Ave., 501-781-3102
tacomama.net

Diablos
528 Central Ave., 501-701-4327
diablostacosandmezcal.com

Capo's Tacos
200 Higdon Ferry Rd., 501-623-8226
capostacos.com

20

MAKE A SPLASH
AT THE WINE BAR

Looking for a *finer* nightlife experience? Venture to Splash Wine Bar for an evening of variety and luxurious ambiance, both indoors and outdoors. With their wide selection of wine, beer, liquor, and food, you won't find yourself lacking in options. And check their website before planning your evening to see what live music they have coming up. The warmly-lit bar pairs well with smooth tunes being performed live in the corner. While indulging, don't hesitate to head to the back of the bar and onto the patio. Secluded from surrounding establishments and filled with firepits, art, and couches, the exterior of Splash is just as luxurious as its interior, if not even more so.

325 Ouachita Ave., 501-701-4544
splashwinebar.com

LOVE THE WINE YOU'RE WITH

AT THE WINERIES

Some say wine is a passport to the world, and when in Hot Springs there are two classic destinations that will delight your palate with locally made wine. At both Winery of Hot Springs and Bathhouse Row Winery, you will sample a variety of wines—for free—and likely fall in love with one enough to leave with a bottle of your own. All made two hours north of Hot Springs out of Altus, Arkansas, these wines are hard to come by outside of these two wineries, as they don't wholesale to liquor stores. This is an opportunity to taste the more sophisticated side of the Natural State. Also, feel free to bring the whole family. For those under 21, there are grape juice tastings available.

Winery of Hot Springs
1503 Central Ave., 501-623-9463
hotspringswinery.com

Bathhouse Row Winery
220 Central Ave., 501-620-4880
hotspringswinery.com

DRINK A CUP OF LOCALLY ROASTED COFFEE

AT RED LIGHT

Just outside of the busiest part of Hot Springs, inside a white house on a hill, there is a quiet, quaint coffee shop known as Red Light Roastery. Inside you will find southern hospitality, comfort, and a cup of locally roasted joe made with local love. Red Light roasts between 300 and 500 pounds of imported coffee beans per week just a few doors down from its shop. So from cold brew to drip to crafted lattés; no matter what concoction you get at Red Light it's guaranteed to be fresh from beans roasted that week. They even offer kombucha on tap. Once there, stay awhile. Sit inside around a table to partake in some board games, or enjoy your beverage outside on the porch surrounded by nature, serenity, and peace. You'll truly feel at home when stopping into Red Light.

1003 Park Ave., 501-609-9357
redlightroastery.com

TIP

While waiting on your order, don't pass up browsing Red Light's gift shop full of unique locally-made items.

MORE WAYS TO COFFEE

Mug Shots
(Drive-thru only)
1331 Airport Rd., Ste. A, 501-693-5677
shotinthemug.com

Kollective
110 Central Ave., 501-701-4000
kollectivecoffeetea.com

Capachi's
600 Garland Ave., 501-538-5528
capachiscoffee.square.site

A Narrow Escape
801 Central Ave., Ste. 34, 501-777-5625
narrowescapear.com

RC Coffee and Collectables
1534 Malvern Ave., Ste. T, 501-359-3555
rccoffeeshopping.com

GET ACQUAINTED
WITH MADAM MAXINE

Maxine Temple Jones was a mountain of a woman residing in Hot Springs in the mid-1900s, working as a madam at one "of the most notorious brothels in one of the most well-known resort towns in the USA," as she states in her memoir *Call Me Madam*. She was spectacular, strong, and audacious, and she lived life to the fullest without a second thought of what Southern society might think of her. She purchased a space on Central Avenue for just $1,000 to have as her brothel, and today that very spot is known as "Maxine's Live." Just like the Madam herself, present-day Maxine's is a place for all to gather and celebrate life. It's a bar, a pizza eatery, and still a dim-lit spot for nightlife fun in the Spa City. Long live the Madam.

700 Central Ave., 501-321-0909
maxineslive.com

OTHER NIGHTLIFE SPOTS TO HIT

Starlite
230 Ouachita Ave.
facebook.com/starlitehotsprings

The Trough
833 Central Ave., 501-701-4390
facebook.com/thetroughbg

Copper Penny Pub
711 Central Ave., 501-622-2570
copper-penny-pub.com

The Big Chill
910 Higdon Ferry Rd., 501-624-5185
chillhotsprings.com

The Malco Lounge
817 Central Ave., 501-623-6200
maxwellblade.com

Ohio Club
336 Central Ave., 501-627-0702
theohioclub.com

VISIT
THE ARGENTINIAN BARS

The Argentinian Coffee and Wine Bar provides refreshments and relaxation at its catch-all location in downtown Hot Springs. You have the options of an oxygen, wine, or coffee bar. The oxygen bar is a 10- to 20-minute session of breathing in oxygen. It's simple, but has incredible benefits like heightening your concentration and calming your nerves. Adults tend to enjoy the therapeutic options at the bar, like "Bliss" or "Zen," and kids tend to enjoy the more fruity scents like "Watermelon" or "Strawberry fields." There is also the wine bar. You may serve yourself at a wine station filled with a variety of wines, 80 percent being Argentinian, or you may sit at the bar and be served. And as for the coffee bar, come to the Argentinian for breakfast or brunch and start your day with one of their coffee creations. Like I said, it's a catch-all location, and one not to be missed.

328 Central Ave., 501-623-2777
facebook.com/coffeewinebar

DINE ON THE DOCK
OF THE WHARF

Step onto the creaky wooden dock of Fisherman's Wharf Steak & Seafood and indulge in some of the finest southern seafood Hot Springs has to offer right there on Lake Hamilton. The environment, the food, the drinks, and the ducks floating by are all in-line with Hot Springs's beloved lake lifestyle. The food is fresh and homegrown, and there's plenty of variety to choose from. But allow me to call your attention to a few of the Wharf's must-tries to get your taste buds tingling. Delectables include the Bang Bang Shrimp, hand-breaded gator, triggerfish (broiled or fried) and the Australian sea bass. And of course, you can't go wrong simply getting your fill from the fresh, raw oyster bar offered at the Wharf.

5101 Central Ave., 501-525-7437
facebook.com/5101spacity

THREE MORE SOUTHERN SEAFOOD EATERIES

Bubba's Catfish
622 Carpenter Dam Rd., 501-262-1100
5411 Central Ave., 501-762-3474
bubbascatfishandseafood.com

Mr. Whiskers
4195 Malvern Ave., 501-262-3474
greatcatfish.com

Cajun Boilers
2806 Albert Pike Rd., 501-767-5695
cajunboilers.com

MUSIC AND ENTERTAINMENT

GET LUCKY
AT OAKLAWN'S CASINO

At Oaklawn Racing Casino Resort, the possibilities are endless. While the term "resort" refers to a more than hundred-million-dollar expansion completed in 2021, don't let the term scare you off if you're just looking for a single night of fun. Hit the casino, and if you're lucky hit a jackpot! There are slots, table games, sports betting, and a high-limits area to choose from. But the gambling is just the start. Enjoy a drink or a meal from one of the numerous bars and restaurants in the casino, with everything from a casual setting at Big Al's Diner, to a five-star dining experience at The Bugler. And of course, in a very Oaklawn-esque fashion the lodging experience is just another form of excellence if you do decide to stay awhile. It's hard to go wrong at Oaklawn, unless you simply don't go.

2705 Central Ave., 501-623-4411
oaklawn.com

TIP

You don't have to enter the casino to dine at Oaklawn, making the restaurants available to all ages.

OAKLAWN DINING AND DRINKING OPTIONS

The Bugler
(Fine dining)
501-363-4790

The First Turn
(Bar, 21+)
501-623-4411

Percs
(Coffee)
501-363-4795

Track Kitchen
(Casual dining)
501-363-4775

Big Al's Diner
(Casual dining)
501-623-4411

EXPERIENCE LIFE AS AN '80S KID

AT THE GALAXY CONNECTION

The Galaxy Connection offers a unique opportunity to reminisce and relive a time that produced arguably the best toys. From the moment you set foot into the museum you're walking down memory lane. This museum for all things 80s, 90s, superheroes, and Star Wars showcases an impressive combination of collectible toys, action figures, trading cards, and fandom art. This place is *dripping* with nostalgia. There is a game room that has video game systems like Atari, Nintendo 64, and Sega. You'll enter an 80s room complete with panel walls decorated with rare trading cards, woven plaid couches, popular toys from the decade, and an 8-track tape playing timely hits to truly set the mood. And there are numerous rooms full of action figures and collectibles like He-Man, G.I. Joe, Marvel and Star Wars characters, fandom-related art, and superhero cosplay suits. Take this rare opportunity to travel back in time while you can.

536 Ouachita Ave., 501-276-4432
thegalaxyconnection.com

TIP

Show up early to your museum reservation to play vintage video and board games in the game room beforehand.

28

TOUR
THE BIGGEST TINY TOWN

For more than 58 years Tiny Town Trains has been a local treasure, capturing the hearts of children and adults alike. Barbara and Chalres Moshinskie describe their attraction as a "model railroad" for lack of a better description, but while there *are* railroads in Tiny Town, that only scratches its surface. Constructed from items like tin cans, coffee lids, toothpicks, and thread spools, Tiny Town is a fully animated culmination of "junk art" and woodwork that represents numerous places and pop culture references from America in the 60s. Come to Tiny Town, look closely, and see if you can spot the tiny Willie Nelson, tiny scene from Gunsmoke, tiny Mount Rushmore, tiny McDonald's or tiny Niagara Falls. Open from March through October, Tiny Town is a place of wonder for children and intrigue for adults.

374 Whittington Ave., 501-624-4742
tinytowntrains.com

BLOW YOUR MIND
AT A MAXWELL BLADE MAGIC SHOW

At a show unlike any other, experience large-scale illusions, close-up magic, comedy, and live music performed by grand illusionist Maxwell Blade and his cast members from the stage of the historic Malco Theatre. This astounding, captivating, and bizarre show lasts about two hours and is entertaining for all ages. Grab some food or candy from the classic theatre concessions stand or head to The Lounge next door for an adult beverage before seating yourself in the 300-seat state-of-the-art venue. Once the show starts, prepare to be amazed, shocked, and stimulated by the bright and flashy tricks and illusions. Blade has been perfecting his craft since the 70s and shocking the masses for decades out of Hot Springs. Maxwell Blade's Theatre of Magic and Comedy has become a notorious local staple, and is a must-see.

817 Central Ave., 501-623-6200
maxwellblade.com

VISIT
THE LOCAL LIBRARY

The Garland County Library is more than just a home to books. It's a connection point for the community, offering educational and entertaining programs, community newspaper archives, and even some art produced by locals. And the library, which is one of the oldest in the state of Arkansas, is not only for local cardholders—it's for anyone. If you are a local, definitely take advantage of the free library card that will provide you access to millions of books (whether physical, digital, or audio), streamed or physical movies, documentaries and TV shows, or even things like fishing poles, cake pans, telescopes or family passes to Mid-America and Garvan Gardens. Not a local eligible for a free card? No worries; nonresidents can get a card for a small annual fee of $30. Want to simply check out a program or movie screening? No card or fee is even necessary.

1427 Malvern Ave., 501-623-4161
gclibrary.com

31

HAVE YOUR PALM READ
BY PSYCHIC LAUREN

Are you looking for guidance in life, love, business, or marriage? We all are, but the answers always seem to lie within. And after all, it was the philosopher Immanuel Kant who said the hand is the visible part of the brain, so consider taking your troubles to Psychic Lauren. This long-time Hot Springs palm reader will review your past, present, and future, helping you uncover the answers your subconscious may be keeping from you. In her very unique building located just outside of the downtown area, you will be taken back to a private room where Psychic Lauren will begin her art of palmistry, reading the physical features of the palm in order to interpret your personality and characteristics, as well as to predict what your future holds. Be certain to call ahead of time to make an appointment, and prepare to find the answers you've been searching for.

1215 Central Ave., Ste. A, 501-623-1210

TWO OTHER PSYCHIC READINGS WORTH YOUR TIME

Tarot and palm readings at The Parlour
340 Ouachita Ave., 501-701-4444
theparlourhs.com

Tarot readings at Historic District Antiques
514 Central Ave., 501-624-3370
antiquesar.com

TAKE A SCENIC DRIVE
THROUGH THE MOUNTAINS

Even in the middle of the busy downtown area of Hot Springs, it's not at all hard to slip away in your vehicle up a winding, tree-lined trail leading you to many overlooks. In your vehicle, cruise up North Mountain off of Fountain Street or West Mountain off of Whittington or Prospect Ave. North Mountain is where you will find the Hot Springs Mountain Tower and a white pagoda where you will look out into the Ouachita Mountains. From West Mountain you will see many different views of the historic downtown below. Prime times to go on both mountains would be sunrise, sunset, or during daylight hours in mid-November to see scenes pretty enough to be in a calendar. But truly, anytime is a good time to take a gander at the mountain views.

CATCH A SHOW
AT THE POCKET THEATRE

If you want to watch a quality live production spawned from the hard work and dedication of a community theatre troupe, clear your schedule for a show at The Pocket Theatre. The theatre is off the beaten path, but through the woods off Park Avenue a cozy, warmly-lit, red theatre house awaits. But what truly warms the heart can be found inside. Every year community members with a genuine love of theatre come together on a volunteer basis to produce a handful of classic plays at a level of quality that will shock you when you realize how little you paid for an admission ticket. No Pocket show is to be missed, as each one showcases some of Hot Springs's top performing arts talent. So make your way down, grab some popcorn, and brace yourself for the showstoppers in-store at every Pocket Theatre production.

170 Ravine St., 501-623-8585
pockettheatre.com

PARTY ON THE LAKE
WITH CAPTAIN JACK

One must experience lake life in order to adequately experience Hot Springs, and there are three beautiful lakes to do it on. But wait, don't have a boat or a boating license? Captain Jack's got your back. Captain Jack's Lake Cruises are a fun and easy way to get that longed-for access to Lake Hamilton. Having been navigating through the waters of Lake Hamilton for over 30 years, Captain Jack is able to get you to the most beautiful spots of the lake—and more importantly keep you from the most dangerous. Get picked from the dock of your choice and hop aboard Captain Jack's 31-foot tritoon boat for a day cruise, sunset cruise, or private charter cruise. Enjoy music and drinks while observing the lake's most scenic views, historic sites and extravagant mansions. If you're lucky, you may even spot a bald eagle along the way. All aboard!

501-547-2743
captainjackslakecruises.com

ONE MORE CRUISE TO CHECK OUT

Belle of Hot Springs
5200 Central Ave., 501-525-4438
belleriverboat.com

35

ADMIRE THE TALENT AND BEAUTY

OF THE FOUL PLAY CABARET

They're beautiful, tattooed, sultry, and dressed to the nines in feathery, flowing outfits (well, for a short time anyway). In fact, their very appropriate slogan is "the only thing hotter than the water in Hot Springs is The Foul Play Cabaret." Allow me to introduce you to the Spa City's very own, and very talented burlesque troupe. No matter the venue, any night spent with these women is one to remember, and it's a chance to see the sheer talent that derives from Hot Springs. Either as a solo, or duo, you'll witness phenomenal and entertaining dances ranging from the decadent 1930s to more modern styles of burlesque. Always look to their website for upcoming shows, but take it from me: if you can catch one on the stage of the historic Central Theatre, that's the way to go.

foulplaycabaret.com

36

CHECK OUT THE BUSKING
IN ADAIR PARK

Locals and drifters alike often take to Kenneth Adair Memorial Park to provide music, dancing, hooping, face painting, caricature drawings, and an array of other entertaining activities for the public. It's not uncommon on a busy Saturday or Sunday for more than one individual or group to perform at the park. This is a place where you can see some of Hot Springs's finest "hidden gem" entertainment. There are even some who set up tables to sell their own handmade items. The park is a beautiful, small section of the downtown area, nestled between merchants. It's complete with a small waterfall fountain, a stage, and numerous benches. The string lights draped above the park make it a well-lit and beautiful scene to enjoy at night, too.

354 Central Ave., 501-321-6871

CHEER ON
THE RUNNING OF THE TUBS

Decorated bathtubs on wheels being raced down the street while thousands dressed in robes and slippers shoot super soakers at them sounds like something straight out of a fever dream, but it's a celebrated reality every year in the Spa City. The Stueart Pennington World Championship Running of the Tubs is a *big deal*, as it celebrates the time people from all over ventured to Hot Springs National Park to bathe in thermal waters thought to have healing properties. Since 2005, every June people have gathered alongside the street in front of Bathhouse Row to cheer on their favorite team dressed in whacky themes and completing even whackier tasks at the request of the judges. Over the years this bathtub race has even grown to acquire ESPN coverage. It's truly unlike anything you will ever experience.

501-321-2277
hotsprings.org

WATCH NINE DAYS
OF DOC FILMS

The Hot Springs Documentary Film Festival is an annual 9-day event that not only champions documentary filmmakers of the south, but also curates a compelling lineup of unforgettable stories from around the world. Celebrated for more than 30 years, HSDFF is the longest-running all-documentary festival in North America and takes place in October at various venues around historic downtown Hot Springs. The festival includes screenings of roughly 100 documentary films along with a range of industry panels and workshops, providing exposure to internationally acclaimed filmmakers and special guests. Whether you're a filmmaker, film-lover, or both, there is something for everyone at this gigantic, luxurious festival. Attend one day or purchase a pass for all 9 days, but whatever you do, don't miss this extraordinary opportunity to kick back and watch some seriously good films produced by some of the best filmmakers of our time.

501-538-0452
hsdfi.org

TIP

The festival is one big party, and by that I mean there is a party every. Single. Night. But they're only available to VIP pass holders. Just food for thought when deciding which route to take in purchasing festival tickets.

39

CELEBRATE LIKE THE IRISH

AT THE WORLD'S SHORTEST ST. PATRICK'S DAY PARADE

Held on Hot Springs's notoriously short 98-foot-long Bridge Street, the city hosts one of the most unique and iconic St. Patrick's Day parades in the world. Since 2004, thousands from near and far have geared up in green to celebrate the jubilant holiday in the Spa City. And don't let the term "shortest" fool you—immense fun is packed into this two-day event. Past celebrity guests have ranged from Mario Lopez to Alfonso Ribeiro to Kevin Bacon, and past concerts have included names like Three Dog Night and Smash Mouth. The community also comes together to create the parade floats you'll see, competing to see whose final product will be the zaniest. It's quirky, it's festive, and it's a whole lot of fun. Out of all St. Patrick's Day celebrations it's one to make a point to experience.

shorteststpats.com

MORE CAN'T-MISS CITYWIDE CELEBRATIONS

Christmas Parade
Downtown Hot Springs

Memorial Day Fireworks
Lake Hamilton

Independence Day Fireworks
Lake Hamilton

Labor Day Fireworks
Lake Hamilton

Martin Luther King Day Parade
Downtown Hot Springs

Veteran's Day Parade
Downtown Hot Springs

hotsprings.org

40

SEE THE HOLIDAY LIGHTS

OF THE CHILI COOK-OFF

Ah, the Tom Daniel Annual Hot Springs Chili Cook-Off. This is truly when the most wonderful time of the year begins in the Spa City. Held on one of the last Mondays of November, this friendly outdoor competition among local businesses is what kicks off the lighting of the holiday lights in downtown Hot Springs. Purchase a ticket, sample all the chili you can get, vote on your favorite, and enjoy good company and music. And at the end of the night, once the switch is flipped, take a stroll and enjoy the thousands of lights decorating downtown. From the giant tree in the parking lot next to the Visitor's Center to the life-sized gingerbread house set up inside The Arlington Resort and Hotel lobby, and everything in between, it's a *magical* sight to see.

128 Exchange St., 501-321-1700

ATTEND
A BRIDGE STREET BLOCK PARTY

Does a block party setting with free concerts, an array of local restaurant food and beverage options, games, and merchants appeal to you? If so, you've got to check out the summer Bridge Street Live! concert series. It's one giant community gathering that provides quality live entertainment right in the middle of the shortest street in Hot Springs. Block parties were popular in Hot Springs years ago, so when the COVID-19 pandemic began to wane and the first-ever Bridge Street Live! concert series was introduced in the summer of 2021, it was once again a gathering people realized they would cherish. Community is the embodiment of BSL!, and it's honestly quite wholesome to see the way people gather, dance, laugh, and play games all evening long during these concert nights. It's an appreciation for the finer things in life, and it can all be found on Bridge Street.

Bridge St., 501-321-2277
hotsprings.org

EMBRACE YOUR FANDOM
AT SPA-CON

Spa-Con is an annual comic convention held in September that appeals to the masses—even those who may have never been acquainted to "con culture" previously—because it's for more than just comic-book lovers. Spa-Con is for the gamers, the cosplayers, the superfans, the artists, the otakus, the collectors, and those who are simply curious! There have been celebrity guests from Rodger Bumpass (the voice actor for Squidward Tentacles in the Nickelodeon series *Spongebob Squarepants*), to Nichelle Nichols (the actress who played Uhura in *Star Trek: The Original Series*). In addition to television celebrities, there are always a slew of famed artists who may have brought to life one of your favorite childhood television or graphic novel characters. So come to Spa-Con and get acquainted with the magic of the quirky, nerdy, and utterly awesome.

134 Convention Blvd., 501-321-2277
spa-con.org

TIP

You'll *definitely* want to dress up as your favorite character when attending this event—it's the right way to con.

43

GLOW ON THE ROW
FOR HALLOWEEN

There are costumes, candy, cupcakes, and more glow sticks than you can count in downtown Hot Springs on Halloween night. This festive site is Glow on the Row; a harvest festival for all ages that provides a fun and family-friendly way to spend part of your All Hallows Eve. While trick-or-treating among downtown merchants you'll find games, fortune telling, face painting, music, costume contests, and more. And some say the downtown historic district is haunted . . . so you may even cross a ghost or two. But whatever you do, don't miss out on one of the thousands of cupcakes provided by Fat Bottomed Girls during the event. This is no trick, just a sweet treat added to this communal Halloween event!

Downtown Hot Springs
501-318-0997

GET YOUR GROOVE ON
AT THE HOT SPRINGS MUSIC FESTIVAL

For decades the annual Hot Springs Music Festival has brought together international musicians each June. It has now grown to host over 100 musicians from several countries each year for over 10,000 attendees to enjoy right here in the Spa City. The Festival pairs world-class mentor musicians from major orchestras, chamber ensembles, and conservatories with especially talented pre-professional apprentices. The result is numerous concerts and open rehearsals performed to the benefit the students, and as entertainment for the audience. This highly distinguished festival has something for everybody as it takes a relaxed approach, hosting its concerts in a variety of non-traditional venues including historic buildings, art galleries, hotel ballrooms, churches, and open-air spaces all around downtown Hot Springs over the course of five days.

501-701-4140
hotmusicfestival.com

A FEW MORE MUSIC FESTIVALS TO CONSIDER

Valley of the Vapors
Independent Music Festival
valleyofthevapors.com

Blues Fest
hotsprings.org

Jazz Fest
hsjazzsociety.org

Hot Water Hills Music and Arts Festival
hotwaterhills.com

SPORTS AND RECREATION

45

MEET GEORGE THE PEACOCK
AT GARVAN WOODLAND GARDENS

Explore the beauty of Garvan Woodland Gardens over its four and a half miles of wooded shoreline and rocky inclines. From the moment you step through the entrance into this lush botanical garden, you're immersed in the beauty of nature. You'll explore numerous seasonal gardens, cross over beautiful bridges, and if you're lucky you may spot George the Peacock or one of his female companions. From the stunning springtime bloom to the wonderland created during the wintertime, there is never a wrong time of year to take a gander at Garvan Gardens. While you're touring, take a load off and grab a bite from the Chipmunk Café. Also, don't forget to swing by the iconic Anthony Chapel before leaving—like everything at the Gardens, it's a beautiful sight.

550 Arkridge Rd., 501-262-9300
garvangardens.org

TIP

Check out the Garvan Gardens website for garden activities like yoga, health walks, and high teas.

46

GET A BETTER LOOK

FROM THE MOUNTAIN TOWER

It's not hard to find beauty all around you in Hot Springs National Park, but the Hot Springs Mountain Tower provides a view you can find nowhere else. This iconic tower sits on Hot Springs Mountain and can be seen from miles away as it stands 216 feet tall. The top of the tower can be accessed via elevator, and its height is what allows incredible 140-mile panoramic views of the Ouachita Mountains, Hot Springs Mountain, and the Diamond Lakes area at 1,256 feet above sea level. But don't discount the views you also get from below while travelling up Hot Springs Mountain to the Mountain Tower. There are two ways to get to the tower: take a beautiful scenic drive to the parking lot, or hike the 1.5 mile trail from Fountain Street.

401 Hot Springs Mountain Dr., 501-881-4020
hotspringstower.com

TIP

After you're done at the Mountain Tower, be sure to check out the views from the white pagoda just slightly downhill from the tower.

GO FULL AUTO
AT MACHINE GUN GROTTO

There are many different ways to experience Hot Springs, and one is to dive into its rich history as a one-time gangster's paradise. And what better way to explore this history than to actually live life as a gangster? In one of the state's largest indoor firing ranges, at Machine Gun Grotto you can shoot a fully automatic Thompson Machine Gun, a firearm made famous by the gangsters of the 1930s. But once you're done living it up as a gangster, give one of their other machine gun options a go—with everything from a .22 to a .308 caliber. These are machines you won't have access to on a daily basis, creating an exhilarating experience as you spray lead across one of the 11 lanes in this two-bay range.

325 Olive St., 501-701-4373
facebook.com/machinegungrotto

MEET THE PIRATES
OF THE COVE

Ahoy, matey! At the only Pirate's Cove course available in Arkansas, putt your way through an 18- or 36-hole mini golf course guarded by lounging pirates. Since 1995 this adventure golf course has been fun for all ages of locals and visitors alike. It's even become a tradition in some families, so if you've never tried your hand at putt-putt at the cove, it definitely makes the Spa City's "must-do" list. In this course, open from Presidents' Day through Thanksgiving, you'll play through mountain caves, across a full-scale pirate ship, over bridges, and under waterfalls—all the while trying not to sink your ball in the flowing streams lining the courses. It's a whole lot of pirate fun for everyone at an incredibly low price.

4612 Central Ave., 501-525-9311
piratescove.net

TWO MORE TO TRY YOUR HAND AT

T-Rex Golf
1115 Central Ave., 501-520-1242
trexgolf.com

Volcano Falls Miniature Golf
2614 Albert Pike Rd., 501-767-8140
funtrackersfamilypark.com

HOP ON A BIKE
AT THE TOURING COMPANY

They say you never forget how to ride a bike. So whether you're an avid rider or haven't picked up a bicycle since you were a kid, visit the Hot Springs Bicycle Touring Company to get on a bike and cruise through the town. At the Bicycle Touring Company you have a few different options. Go on a guided tour that takes you to multiple springs in the National Park, or one that takes you through the art installations on the Hot Springs Creek Greenway trail. Or simply rent a bike and venture out on your own! There are numerous biking trails close to the Company's location just outside of downtown, and some will lead you to the Northwoods Trail System, which has trails galore for anyone looking to do mountain biking from easy to extreme.

436 Broadway St., 501-276-2175
hotspringsbicycletouringco.com

BIKE THE NORTHWOODS

The Northwoods Trail System is relatively new to Hot Springs, but it has added miles of biking and hiking fun to the town. It's also located about five minutes outside of the busy downtown, yet is a quiet oasis to escape into nature. For bikers there are three levels of trails. Look for the black markers for a challenge, the blue markers for a mild ride and the green markers for the easier rides. Want to ride with a group? There are multiple "no drop" (meaning no rider gets left behind) group riding activities, including the annual Gudrun Festival and the monthly full moon rides. To keep up with the growth of this trail system and its activities, always visit its website before planning your visit.

501-321-2027
northwoodstrails.org

ONE MORE BIKING DESTINATION

Hot Springs Creek Greenway Trailhead
118 Orange St.
cityhs.net

TIP

The hours of the Northwoods Trails are 6 a.m. to 10 p.m., and there are three trailheads to access the system. Waterworks, which is the main trailhead, is located at 300 Pineland Drive; Pullman is located at 300 Pullman Avenue, Cedar Glades is located at 461 Wildcat Road; and Bull Bayou is located at 1124 Cedar Glades Road.

51

MAKE
A NARROW ESCAPE

Do you perform well under pressure? Put your mind to the test at A Narrow Escape by solving a series of puzzles in order to escape from one of these multi-level, one-hour escape rooms. But wait, there's more to this unique establishment. In addition to escape rooms, you will find a full-blown game deck on the exterior. Put yourself in the Robot Battle Arena, where you and up to three friends can battle each other to the death as robots. Keep the competition going and hit up the Robo Karts afterward. Then work together to escape from the Human Zoo—a zoo the robots put the humans in (after taking over the world, of course). You'll have five minutes to solve a series of puzzles to convince the robots you, too, are a robot so they will set you free. But wait, there's *more*! Before leaving ANE, be sure to treat yourself to a coffee and ice cream for all your hard work at the endearing coffee shop set up in the lobby.

801 Central Ave., Ste. 34, 501-777-5625
narrowescapear.com

ONE MORE ESCAPE ROOM TO CHECK OUT

Escape Hot Springs
622 Malvern Ave., 501-463-6532
escapehotsprings.com

TIP
Can't get enough robot fun?
Check out A Narrow Escape's "Robo World"
across the street at 810 Central Avenue.

GET EDUCATED
AT MID-AMERICA SCIENCE MUSEUM

Mid-America Science Museum has a little bit of everything for all ages, but the “sweet spot” is for those in the second to sixth grade. It’s a hands-on science museum that has been educating Hot Springs since 1979, mostly through the physical sciences, but there is some nature science, and *definitely* some dinosaurs. One exhibit that’s a must-see at the museum is the iconic Tesla Coil Show. This Tesla Coil holds the world record for being the world’s most powerful conical Tesla Coil at 1 and a half million volts. The museum also offers a digital dome with a 360-degree video experience that can be a planetarium or any other kind of scene you can think of. After embarking on exploration of everything the museum’s interior holds, venture outside and walk the Dinotrek to see replica dinosaurs on the nature trail. Mid-America is a place for anyone to explore the wonder of science and have a lot of fun doing so.

500 Mid America Blvd., 501-767-3461
midamericamuseum.org

53

PET A GATOR
AT THE FARM

The Arkansas Alligator Farm and Petting Zoo is a fond memory of nearly anyone who grew up in the southern or central part of the state, and it continues to delight children and adults to this day. Founded in 1902, it bills itself as the oldest attraction in Hot Springs. Visit the farm for an opportunity to hold a baby alligator; feed and pet emus, pigmy goats, and sheep; feed parakeets; see wolves, mountain lions, raccoons, turkeys, wild ducks, peacocks, and monkeys; and feed alligators with meat on a stick during feeding season. (Alligator feeding times are at noon Thursday, Saturday, and Sunday from May through October.) The Alligator Farm is a place for children to explore an environment with animals they have likely never been so close to before, but it's also a place for adults to feel like kids again.

847 Whittington Ave., 501-623-6172
alligatorfarmzoo.com

54

BRUNCH AND BATHE
AT THE ARLINGTON

The Arlington Resort Hotel and Spa has been a Hot Springs staple since 1875. Having hosted guests like Theodore Roosevelt, Babe Ruth, and Al Capone, the historic hotel has made an impressive name for itself. However, if you're in Hot Springs but aren't staying as a guest at The Arlington, there are other ways to experience it. Plan a day to brunch and bathe here. Brunch, held only on Sundays in the Venetian Dining Room, features a spread of foods like crepes, french toast, and omelets, and of course it won't be lacking mimosas or bloody mary's. Afterward, hit the Arlington Bathhouse. You will get a classic bathhouse experience, providing you with a private bath and bather who will give you a thorough scrub down. Leave feeling full and rejuvenated, ready to enjoy the rest of your day in the Spa City as you exit the doors of one of its most historically treasured buildings.

239 Central Ave., 501-623-7771
arlingtonhotel.com

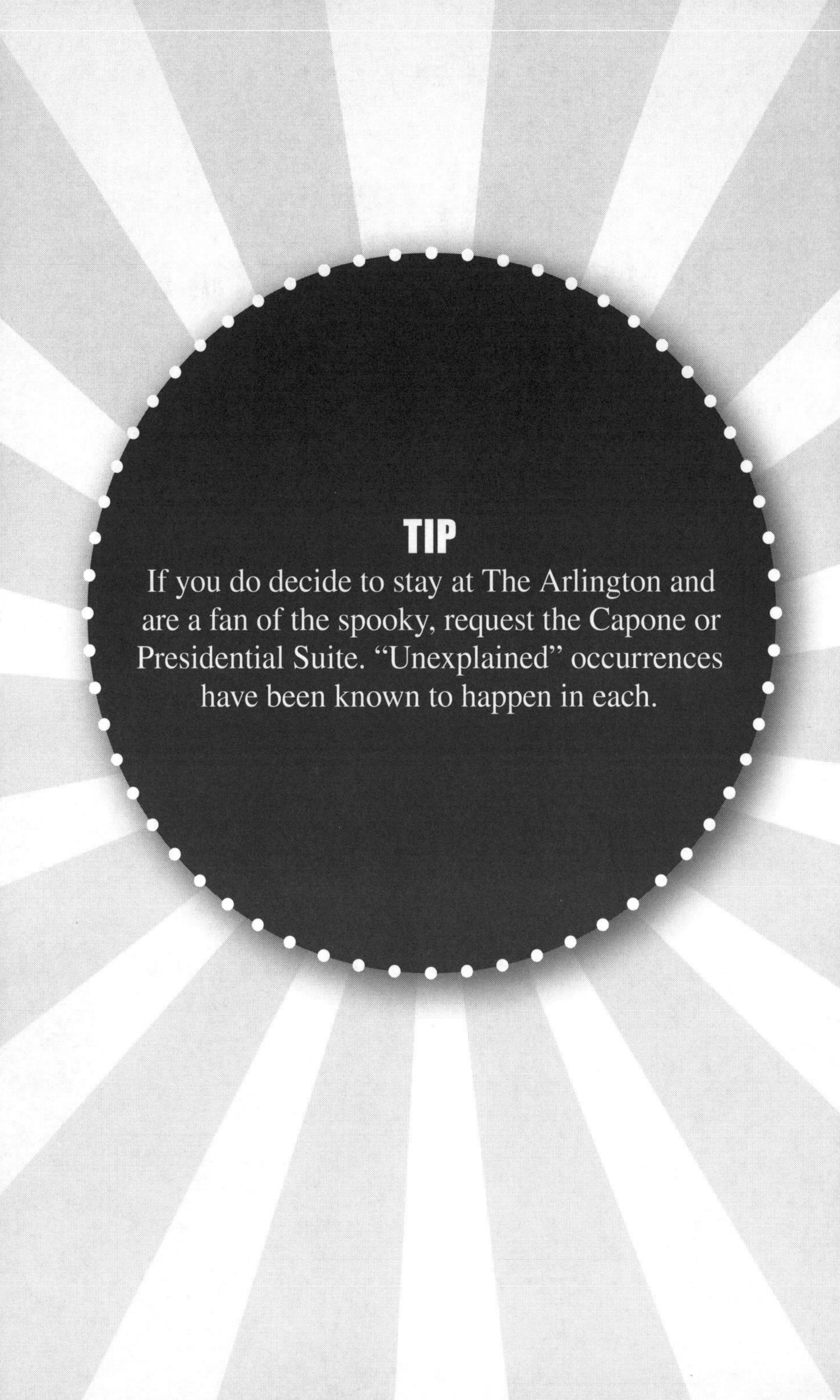
TIP
If you do decide to stay at The Arlington and are a fan of the spooky, request the Capone or Presidential Suite. "Unexplained" occurrences have been known to happen in each.

55

SWIM
AT LAKE OUACHITA STATE PARK

Lake Ouachita State Park has many beautiful spots for hiking and camping, but one thing you've got to make time to do when visiting the park is take advantage of its many swimming holes in the summertime. Lake Ouachita is arguably one of the cleanest lakes in the area, and this is no secret. So even though there are many swimming holes, arrive early before the good ones fill up (ahem, the sandy beach of Three Sisters Springs). Also, bring plenty of water and snacks; the swimming areas are fairly far from any food or drink establishments. And a word to the wise: wait until mid-summer to give the water time to warm up. A mid-morning and afternoon spent at Lake Ouachita makes for a perfect summer's day.

5451 Mountain Pine Rd., 501-767-9366
arkansasstateparks.com

BREAK INTO YOUR CREATIVE SIDE

AT EMERGENT ARTS

Emergent Arts is a great place for emerging artists—kids and adults alike—to get their hands dirty, explore their creativity, and admire the work and processes of other artists. Locals can submit to gallery exhibits, view artwork on display anytime, take multi-session classes, and join the studio membership program. Visitors are welcome to drop by the gallery to view the current exhibits and artwork by local students. There is also the option of partaking in one of Emergent Arts' one-time workshops. Classes and workshops are taught by professional artists and include dance and movement, creative writing, and many 2-D and 3-D visual art processes. The beauty of Emergent Arts is that you don't have to be a professional artist to try your hand in the art scene. It's a safe haven for expression, creativity, inclusivity, and diversity.

341-A Whittington Ave., 501-613-0352
emergentarts.org

DIG FOR TREASURE
AT RON COLEMAN'S

When in Hot Springs you'll see countless shops carrying crystals, but what's all the hubbub? Well, the Ouachita Mountains surrounding Hot Springs are where some of the world's largest deposits of quartz crystals can be found. It just takes a little digging and luck to find one. Think you can unearth some quartz crystals of your own? Give it a try at Ron Coleman Mining, where they guarantee you'll dig up enough quartz to cover the cost of digging, or else you'll receive a credit to use in their gift shop. This unique opportunity to get dirty and dig around for a chance to unearth literal treasure is a must-do for anyone in the Hot Springs area.

155 Crystal Ridge Ln., Jessieville, AR 71949, 501-984-5396
colemanquartz.com

VISIT THE WATERFALL
AT LAKE CATHERINE

Lake Catherine State Park is a quiet and beautiful oasis centered around Lake Catherine, and it features one of the only natural waterfalls in the area. To get to this 10-foot flowing beauty, you can take a rugged 1.6 mile hike or a 10-minute walk from the parking lot. Choose your fate, but know that underneath the waterfall is a commonly used swimming hole where you can cool off no matter which route you take. To start the journey, travel to the Falls Branch Trailhead. From there, take a right to get on the mildly challenging hiking trail, or a left to get on the easy-going dirt walking trail. Bring the kids, bring the dogs, and most importantly bring a water bottle and camera for when you make it to the waterfall.

1200 Catherine Park Rd., 501-844-4176
arkansasstateparks.com

FOLLOW THE RED BRICK ROAD
OF THE GRAND PROMENADE

Once used as a place for spa-goers to exercise after receiving their thermal water treatments in the bathhouses, the Grand Promenade now serves as a scenic walk. It is located directly above Bathhouse Row, and can be easily accessed from Reserve Street, from Fountain Street, or up the staircase between the Fordyce and Maurice Bathhouses. While on the Grand Promenade, observe the beauty that surrounds you, picnic on the grassy hill, dive more into the history of the Promenade with the plaques located along the path, or stray onto one of the marked trails branching off the red brick road that will lead you up Hot Springs Mountain or down to Central Avenue. Whatever you do, don't visit Downtown Hot Springs without venturing up to experience the Promenade if you've never had the pleasure.

501-620-6715

HIKE

THE GULPHA GORGE TRAIL

Hiking compliments Hot Springs just as well as thermal water does. However, with a plethora of choices in hiking trails, the Gulpha Gorge Trail should make the top, or close to it, of any hiker's wish-list. This moderate hike up a mountain is 1.2 miles in length round-trip and will take you on a scenic journey. Begin by parking at the Gulpha Gorge Campground, and access the trailhead by crossing Gulpha Creek. While crossing the creek, look to your right and you'll find the iconic small concrete arch bridge that is often seen in images showcasing Hot Springs. Once the hike begins, the first half is steep, so you'll gain height quickly as you wind up the mountain, and the higher you get, the more intriguing the lookout is. The trail will lead you to Hot Springs Mountain Trail and Goat Rock Trail, allowing you to decide whether to elongate your hike or head back down the mountain.

101 Reserve St., 501-620-6715
alltrails.com

ESCAPE
TO HOLLYWOOD PARK

Even Arkansas has a Hollywood; see for yourself. Take a walk through Hollywood Park and allow yourself to escape into its whimsy. From the giant wood-carved wizard to the stone castle-like structures, this park is reminiscent of a far away land. Shaded by trees, you'll walk along this beautiful park observing artistic structures placed throughout and crossing over streams. There is also playground equipment, so bring your little one—whether that's an actual child or your inner-child. Also pack a lunch and stay awhile, enjoying the beauty and art surrounding while you dine at one of the park's tables or under one of its gazebos. Still haven't gotten enough of the great outdoors after visiting Hollywood? No worries; take a stroll on the Greenway Trail located in front of the park. Hang a right on the trail when exiting the park for a more scenic walk, or a left to access an outdoor workout area.

400–425 Hollywood Ave.

SIX OTHER PARKS TO CHECK OUT

Family Park
215 Family Park Rd., 501-321-6871
cityhs.net

Whittington Park
Whittington Ave.
nps.gov

Entergy Park
530 Lake Park Dr., 501-321-6871
cityhs.net

Kimery Park
271 Kimery Ln., 501-321-6871
cityhs.net

David F. Watkins Memorial Park
811 Park Ave.
cityhs.net

Cedar Glades Park
461 Wildcat Rd., 501-623-2854
garlandcounty.org

PLAY IN THE TREES
AT ADVENTUREWORKS

From zip line tours to an extensive ropes course, Adventureworks Hot Springs won't leave you anything less than exhilarated and adrenaline rushed. Zip lining, recommended for those 8 years and older, comes in several varieties at Adventureworks. Take the tour and experience 10 zip lines as you're rushed through the forest alongside Tributary Creek, which feeds Lake Catherine. There are also multiple seasonal courses, like a haunted zip line conducted at nighttime for Halloween, or a sweetheart zip line that rides two for Valentine's Day. The ropes course, recommended for those ages 12 and up, is a Treetop Aerial Adventure 16-element challenge course made up of swinging bridges, hanging vines, and cargo nets. Now go have a little fun and maybe try something new at Adventureworks.

1700 Shady Grove Rd., 501-262-9182
adventureworks.com

BLOW OFF SOME STEAM
AT BIG AXE BATTLEGROUND

Life got you down? Ever want to just pick up an axe and throw it with all the strength you can muster? Make those violent dreams come true at the Big Axe Battleground (where safety is first, followed by fun!) Whether you're there for team building, a party, or just a night out with friends, rent a lane at Big Axe and take turns throwing an axe at 10 wooden targets. No prior experience? Don't fret, there's an on-site instructor to help you become a pro in no time. You'll be in for a night of fun, competition, and quite honestly a workout. Also, to make it a real party the Big Axe is a BYOB (bring your own beer) establishment. So gear up in your best pair of closed-toed shoes, leave the kids younger than 14 at home, and get ready to chuck some sharp objects.

500 Ouachita Ave., 501-596-8600
bigaxebattlegrounds.com

SEE

WHAT DESTINATIONS AWAIT YOU

Hot Springs is known as the Spa City for its bathhouses, but there are many ways to "spa" in this city. At Destinations Day Spa you will have an opportunity to escape from the daily stresses of life and to the ultimate destination of zen from the moment you walk through their doors. In this more contemporary spa, you will have seven "destinations" to choose from, where ambiance is set through music, art, aroma, and attitude. With an array of services like body rituals, massages, facials, an oxygen bar, spray tans, waxing, and lash and brow, you won't leave Destination's anything less than calm, relaxed, and rejuvenated. Go on, explore all sides of spa-ing in the Spa City.

250 Cornerstone Blvd., 501-525-3400
hsdestinationsdayspa.com

A FEW MORE SPAS WORTH YOUR TIME

Thai-Me
328 Central Ave., 501-520-0100
thai-me.com

Chrysalis
4332 Central Ave., 501-520-5400
chrysalisdayspa.com

Spa Botanica (Embassy Suites)
400 Convention Blvd., 501-321-4444
spabotanicahotsprings.com

Astral Spa (Oaklawn)
2705 Central Ave., 501-363-4670
oaklawn.com

TAKE A KAHUNA BAY PONTOON
ON LAKE HAMILTON

When in Hot Springs, you may take a look out at the lake and see the sun sparkling on the water and want nothing more than to be out on it with fellow boaters sailing those waters. Well, make it happen by renting a pontoon boat from Kahuna Bay to explore Lake Hamilton on your own. From April to November one of these 150-horsepower motorized pontoons seating up to 10 people are available for rent. Crank up the fun and add on one of K-Bay's inner tube rentals. Once rented, the pontoon is yours for a minimum of four hours—so take hold, drive responsibly, and see what all 27 miles of that beautiful water have to offer.

4904 Central Ave., Ste. A, 501-520-5700
kahunabay.com

TIP

If you weren't born in 1985 or before, you must present a boater's license prior to renting.

MORE PLACES TO RENT FROM

Hot Springs Marina
301 Lakeland Dr., 501-525-7776
hotspringsmarina.com

Gregg Orr Marine
4903 Central Ave., 501-525-1818
greggorrmarineandrv.com

Salty Dog
4931 Central Ave., 501-525-7007
saltydogboatingcenter.com

Marineland
1318 Airport Rd., 501-767-4144

MAKE A SPLASH
AT MAGIC SPRINGS THEME AND WATER PARK

Magic Springs Theme and Water Park may just give you one of the most fun days you'll ever spend in Hot Springs, and this is not an exaggeration. Set an entire day aside and start your trip in Magic Springs' amusement park. Get your adrenaline pumping with rides like the Gauntlet, X-Coaster, Brain Drain, and Plummet Summit. Afterward, cool off and head to the water park. You'll find countless water slides for both the fun and thrill-seekers. There are also more calm approaches if you'd like to just spend your day in the lazy river or wave pool. Go on the right day and you can end your trip to the park with a concert at the amphitheater. The park caters to multiple age groups, so there's a little something for everyone to enjoy at Magic Springs.

1701 E Grand Ave., 501-624-0100
magicsprings.com

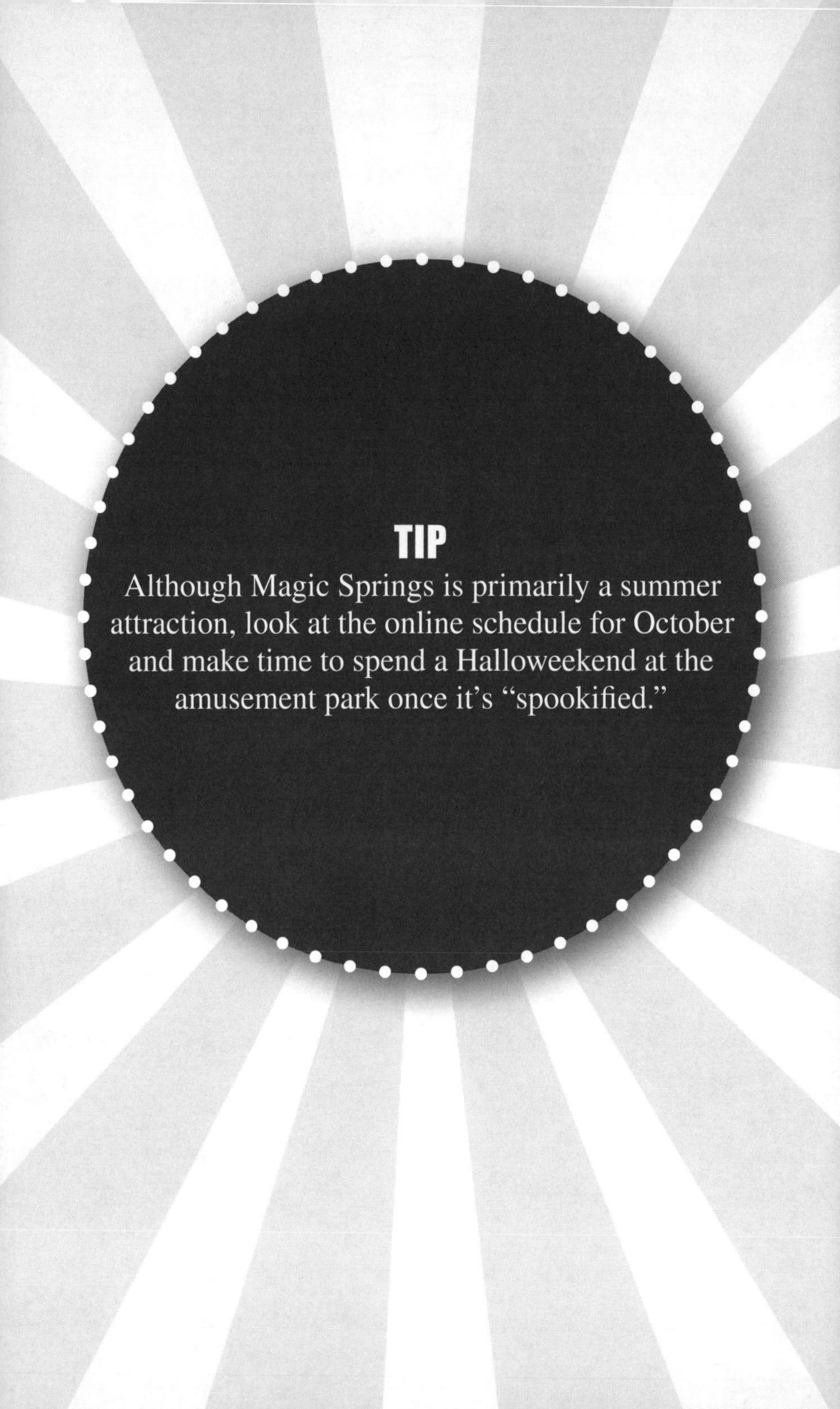
TIP
Although Magic Springs is primarily a summer attraction, look at the online schedule for October and make time to spend a Halloweekend at the amusement park once it's "spookified."

GO DOWN TO THE FAIRGROUNDS

FOR SOME OUTDOOR FUN

Once upon a time, fairgrounds were happening spots for all kinds of events year-round within communities, and were the obvious spot for local fairs. However, over the years these outdoor venues have tended to die down and, as a result, lack in quality. However, this simply isn't the case for the Garland County Fairgrounds, which has relatively new facilities and fun events happening regularly. At the local fairgrounds you can catch the longest-running demolition derby in Arkansas in April; an annual fair complete with a carnival, rodeo, and livestock competition held in September; the only renaissance fair in the state in November; concerts; monster truck rallies' and so much more. In some places, fairgrounds may be a thing of the past, but the one in Garland County is alive, well, and growing.

4831 Malvern Ave., 501-412-5794
garlandcountyfair.com

PLACE A BET ON A KENTUCKY DERBY HOPEFUL

IN THE ARKANSAS DERBY

The Arkansas Derby is one of the most anticipated events held in the state each year, and it happens right here at Oaklawn Racing Casino Resort. Dress in your finest clothing, top yourself with a traditionally extravagant Derby Day hat, bring any tokens that may give you luck, and head down to Oaklawn four weeks before the first Saturday in May. Watch from the stands or infield as Kentucky Derby hopefuls race around the track, and bet on a pony or two. From the infield, enjoy not only the view, but the party. Complete your experience by enjoying live music, cold beer, the traditional corned beef sandwiches that come along with Derby Day, and hopefully a *big win*.

2705 Central Ave., 501-623-4411
oaklawn.com

TIP

You don't have to wait on Derby Day to enjoy the races at Oaklawn. Racing runs the weekends of December through May. The full schedule with purse amounts can be found on the Oaklawn website.

SALOON
WILDCAT MINE FOR 2ALE CHEEP FERCA2H
OPEN ALL NITE
DU GANG2TER MU2IUM UVA MERICA HOT 2PRING2, ARKANZAW
2HERIF'2 OFFICE
DRINKS FER MONEY NOT FER THE BULL
OLD CORNO FRESH DAILY 4 BITS
CAFE-OPEN REER ROOM
GAMBLING ROOM DOWNSTA NO DRINKS SE
IN-HAPPY-HOLLO
NO PARKING

CULTURE AND HISTORY

QUAFF THE ELIXIR
OF THE PARK

At an average of 143-degrees fahrenheit, the thermal water flowing from the hot springs in Hot Springs National Park is safe to drink, and has been coveted since the Native Americans found it, labeling the area "Valley of the Vapors." They enjoyed its healing properties in peace, and over time it began to attract the masses. Today, Hot Springs's thermal waters continue to draw people from all over the world as it's still thought by some to have medicinal properties. But regardless of what stance you take on the water's abilities, it's a rite of passage to at least taste or touch the water when you find yourself in Hot Springs. This can be done at one of the fountain or pool locations downtown. Also, when downtown feel free to stop any park rangers you may see walking Bathhouse Row or working out of the Fordyce Bathhouse for more on the history of the waters.

Downtown Hot Springs

VISIT
BATHHOUSE ROW

Bathhouse Row is the line of eight beautiful stone and brick Victorian-style bathhouses located in the heart of downtown Hot Springs. However, while they're all technically bathhouses, only two operate as such today. To bathe, soak and relax in the thermal waters of a bathhouse, visit the Quapaw or Buckstaff. The Quapaw is the only one of the two with a large thermal water public pool to relax in, while both have a private bath option. If you want to see how bathing used to be done in the "olden days," visit the free three-story museum in the Fordyce (so impressive it requires its own entry on this list, which can be found on the next page). The house also serves as the National Park Visitor's Center. The Lamar is now an emporium, the Ozark is a cultural center, and the Maurice is currently closed, as of 2021. The last two houses are Hale and Superior, which have been transformed into dining establishments (and Hale as a hotel, too) both mentioned in the food section. And there you have it: a short guide through the houses to get the most out of your experience on the Row.

Downtown Hot Springs

71

SEE HOW THE BATHING USED TO BE DONE
AT THE FORDYCE BATHHOUSE

The Fordyce Bathhouse, opened on March 1, 1915, is the largest bathhouse on the row and was the first house to go out of business (on June 30, 1962). Today, it's back open and holds a three-story museum inside, offering free self-guided tours to show you just how the bathing used to be done. The bathhouse culture of Hot Springs is widely known, but the bathing experience you get in the Quapaw and Buckstaff houses today aren't quite the same as how they used to get clean and pampered back in the day. To see what once was, step back in time to this fully preserved bathhouse. See the vintage contraptions used to promote healing and relaxation, the fully equipped gym on the top floor, and other items like period clothing and accessories that have been preserved for over a century. This unique experience allows you to relive a large part of what Hot Springs was and is known for around the world.

369 Central Ave., 501-620-6715

72

MEET ANOTHER KIND OF SPRING WATER
AT MOUNTAIN VALLEY SPRING CO.

When you ask about Hot Springs, you get a slew of information about the thermal waters derived from the national park, but don't overlook the mountain valley spring water. It's also found within the national park, but comes from 12 miles outside of the city. Mountain Valley Spring Company has been collecting and distributing this water out of Hot Springs for over 150 years in its unique glass jugs and green bottles. You may have even seen it in grocery stores across the world, as the company ships internationally. This 7.8 pH water is naturally rich in minerals like calcium, magnesium, and potassium, but its historical properties are just as valuable. Stop by the company to tour its free museum on the second floor to learn more of why this spring water was and is valued similarly to the thermal spring water.

150 Central Ave., 501-246-8017
mountainvalleyspring.com

73

LEARN ABOUT HOT SPRINGS'S OUTLAW PAST

AT THE GANGSTER MUSEUM OF AMERICA

Believe it or not, one facet of Hot Springs's celebrated history includes illegal activities like gambling, drinking, and prostitution, which drew in infamous criminals from around the world. Big gangster names like Owney Madden, Al Capone, John Dillinger, and Lucky Luciano, along with outlaws like Bonnie and Clyde, Pretty Boy Floyd, and Creepy Kripas all made their way to Hot Springs during their lifetimes. Some came for just a season to escape from the law, and some kept returning for decades. The history behind Hot Springs's gangsters is so intriguing that once you scratch the surface you'll long to know more. Luckily, there's one museum in the heart of Downtown Hot Springs that conducts a deep dive, answering all of your most burning questions. Spend an hour touring the eight galleries inside The Gangster Museum of America to enlighten yourself about this rich and scandalous history of Hot Springs.

510 Central Ave., 501-318-1717
tgmoa.com

TIP
Want more gangster history?
Visit the Josephine Tussaud Wax Museum
or the Garland County Historical Society.

EXPLORE THE RUINS
OF THE ABANDONED CHEWAUKLA BOTTLING FACTORY

The thing about abandoned ruins in the Natural State is that it doesn't take too long for anything to be reclaimed by nature, giving once-populated structures a second life and a different kind of beauty. It's unknown when the Chewaukla Bottling Factory was abandoned, but what's left of it now is a wonder. Allow me to help you discover the ruins of this abandoned factory. There's no set address for the site, but here's some navigation that will help: Head up Park Avenue from downtown Hot Springs; take a right onto Gorge Road; from there, take a left on Sleepy Valley Road; at around 515 Sleepy Valley Road you will pass a small bridge, and the ruins will be on your right, just through the trees. Enjoy their beauty, and respect their remains while visiting.

Sleepy Valley Road
abandonedar.com

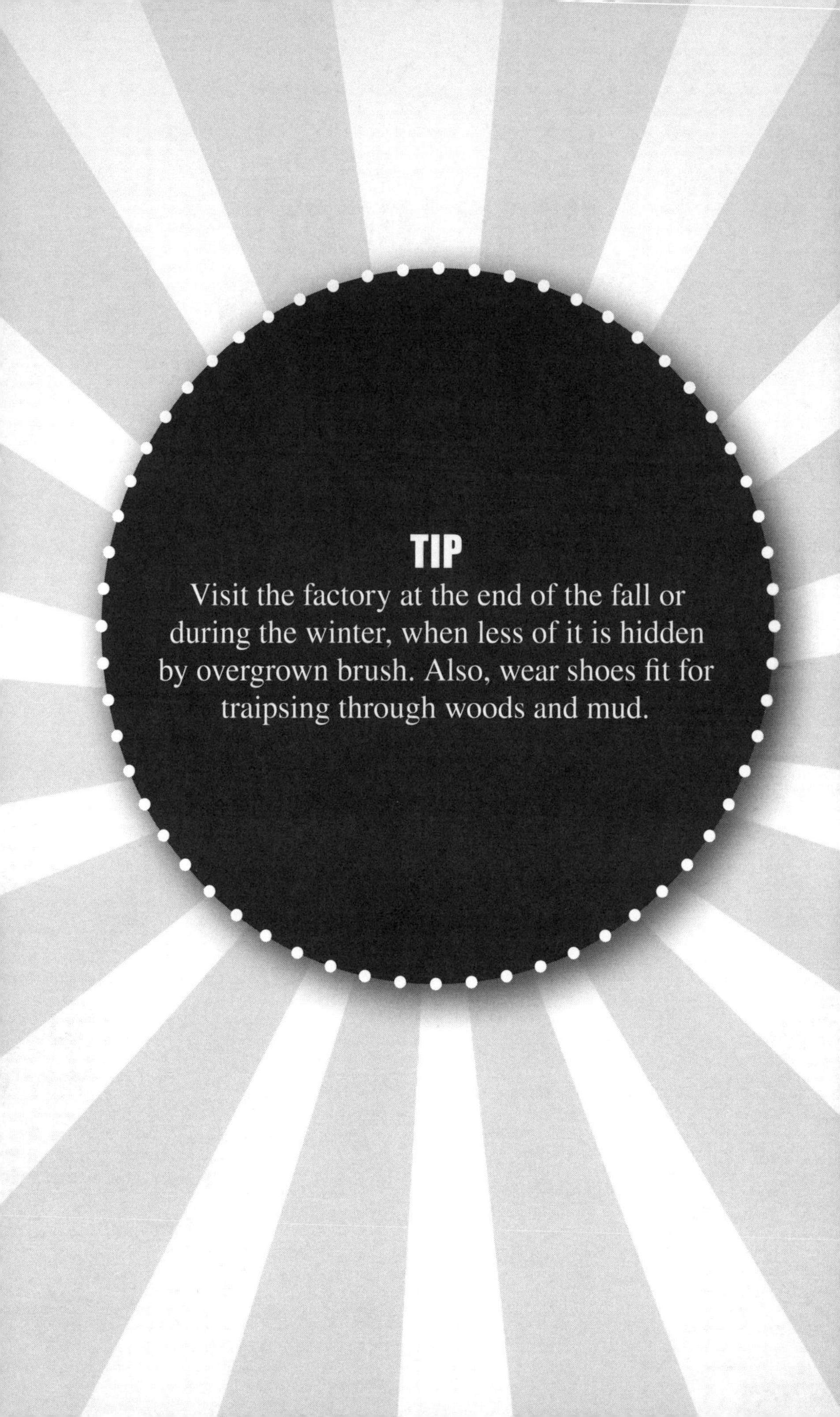
TIP
Visit the factory at the end of the fall or during the winter, when less of it is hidden by overgrown brush. Also, wear shoes fit for traipsing through woods and mud.

HEAR LOCAL GHOST STORIES
ON THE HAUNTED WALKING TOURS

Haunts, mysteries, murders, ghosts, deaths, suicides . . . every town has an abundance of infamous eerie stories from its past, and there's one outlet in Hot Springs that reveals all—even things most locals may not know (or may just wish they didn't know). The Haunted Walking Tours of downtown Hot Springs dive into facts, myths, and legends for one hour every night, starting at 8 p.m. The tour guide will take you to many historic buildings thought to be haunted, telling you of the dark secrets hiding in both Hot Springs's past and present. There are no reservations needed; just show up at 430 Central Ave. dressed appropriately for the weather and for walking, and purchase your tickets up to 30 minutes prior to the start of the tour.

430 Central Ave., 501-339-3751
hotspringshauntedtours.com

76

GET ACQUAINTED WITH THE HISTORIANS

OF THE HISTORICAL SOCIETY

There is so much history within Hot Springs, Arkansas, that it's impossible for any one person to know it all. However, there is a group of individuals with an impressive archival system who pride themselves in sharing their knowledge with curious minds. Take a visit to the Historical Society of Garland County and flip through their thousands of archives—both digital and physical—to learn more about the history of pretty much anything in the Spa City. And utilize not only the archival system, but the archivists. The historical society is run and organized by numerous dedicated volunteer historians who are there to assist you in your look back into history.

328 Quapaw Ave., 501-321-2159
garlandcountyhistoricalsociety.com

77

HOP ON A TROLLEY

FOR A TOUR

Get shown around town by Hot Springs Trolley Tours. In these classic-looking, air conditioned trolleys—run on the road rather than a standard tram track—you'll experience beautiful sites and historical landmarks, and you'll get recommendations on all the fun things to do here. Once the tour begins, you will venture into the scenic mountains of Hot Springs. But that's just the start of this one hour and 20 minute journey. The tour will take you to countless historical sites and through neighborhoods lined with homes built in the 1800s and early 1900s. Along the way you'll also be directed to numerous can't-miss attractions throughout the city. Your driver will narrate your tour so you don't miss a thing as you casually roll through town on these iconic green and gold trolleys.

706 Central Ave., 501-701-4410
hotspringstrolley.com

ONE MORE TOUR TO TRY

National Park Duck Tours
418 Central Ave., 501-321-2911
seehotsprings.com

78

ENTER A WORLD OF WAX
AT THE JOSEPHINE TUSSAUD WAX MUSEUM

Wax museums are timeless, and each has something new to offer. At Hot Springs's World of Wax at the Josephine Tussaud Wax Museum, you will walk among various past presidents, celebrities, historical figures, Disney characters, horror film characters, and even a life-size scene of The Last Supper. There are over 100 figures in total to admire, take photos with, and learn about as you take this self-guided tour. The museum, which has been a mainstay in Hot Springs since 1967, was once known as the Southern Club. This was one of the clubs in the city's illegal gambling era that numerous infamous gangsters flocked to, and to pay homage to this the museum has more recently added a gambling museum to its product. There is much history to be seen and learned here in this Hot Springs staple.

Josephine Tussaud Wax Museum
250 Central Ave., 501-623-5836
seehotsprings.com

STROLL THROUGH
THE WALK OF FAME

Hot Springs's "Arkansas Walk of Fame," established in 1996, honors people who were born or lived in Arkansas and made a significant contribution in their field. As of 2021 there are 65 black plaques decorating the sidewalk, starting in front of the Visitor's Center, located at 629 Central Ave. As families nominate their loved ones, more plaques are added annually. When browsing, you may come across names of people you had no idea came from Arkansas. A few you'll see include author and poet Maya Angelou, who was born in Stamps, Arkansas; actor Jerry Van Dyke, who resided in Glenrose, Arkansas; and Walmart founder Sam Walton, who resided in Bentonville, Arkansas. The tribute gives just a taste of the unique ties the state has to idols celebrated around the world.

The corner of Central Avenue and Spring Street

WALK
THE HISTORIC BASEBALL TRAIL

Hot Springs has a rich history in baseball, as it was the site of one of the first spring training locations for major league teams. World-renowned players like Babe Ruth, Cy Young, Hank Aaron, and Jackie Robinson (just to name a few) played preseason games in the Spa City. They spent their time not only playing ball, but also bathing in the thermal waters and relaxing at some of their favorite hotels. Now, through the Hot Springs Historic Baseball Trail, using your phone you can take a self-guided tour to learn more of this history while you visit the actual sites where these world famous players spent time. From Whittington Avenue to Shady Grove Road, there are 32 green plaques on this trail that take you on a journey back in time, bringing history to life.

1215 Whittington Ave., 501-321-6871
hotspringsbaseballtrail.com

81

TAKE
A HORSE-DRAWN CARRIAGE RIDE

Get back to the "olden" days and depart from the historic Arlington Hotel in a horse-drawn carriage. There are two paths to be taken on this 20-minute ride, each with historical narration by the carriage driver. One path takes you on a quiet, romantic ride through Whittington Park. The other takes you past Bathhouse Row and to the old train depot, and is more focused on history. Running every night it doesn't rain from Memorial to Labor Day, the carriage rides run on a first-come, first-served basis. For two adults the cost is $30, and an additional $5 for every person added after that. Up to seven adults or 10 small children can fit on one carriage. After Labor Day, the carriage rides are only offered on Friday and Saturday evenings. It's an opportunity not common to come by in Arkansas, so you won't want to miss this unique historical tour.

239 Central Ave., 501-520-9955

ATTEND THE LONGEST CONTINUOUSLY RUNNING WEDNESDAY NIGHT POETRY

Regardless of the weather, and even during a global pandemic; since Feb. 1, 1989, Wednesday Night Poetry has been held across various venues in downtown Hot Springs and virtually without missing a single Wednesday of poetry reading. The weekly readings, currently held in Kollective Coffee+Tea free of charge, provide a place to give locals and visitors of any age to express themselves in a room of kindred spirits. Starting at 6:30 p.m., an open mic for all poets, songwriters, and storytellers starts things off, and at 7 p.m. featured poets that include local, regional, or touring artists do a 20 to 30 minute set. This is followed by a second round of open mic. Come to listen or come to pour your heart out; either way, WNP will have a seat waiting for you.

110 Central Ave.
facebook.com/wednesdaynightpoetry

ADMIRE LOCAL ART
ON A GALLERY WALK

Hot Springs's art culture is thriving and impressive for a town of its size, and on the first Friday evening of every month this art scene is showcased in a communal Gallery Walk. The event is a time to tour numerous galleries scattered throughout downtown, and perhaps even come away with an original artwork or two. Dress up if you'd like, dress down if you'd like, but most importantly dress for the weather because since August 1989, the Gallery Walk has been held in rain, shine, sleet or snow. Existing and pop-up art galleries use this time to debut new exhibits, and sometimes there is even a meet-and-greet with the featured artists. Galleries will keep their doors open to the public later than usual, and some even extend that hospitality to serving wine and other refreshments. It's a monthly party, and everyone's invited! No RSVP necessary.

Downtown Hot Springs
hotspringsarts.org

TIP

Plan out your Gallery Walk route ahead of time by visiting hotspringsarts.org to see participating galleries, featured exhibits, and hours of operation for individual stops.

A FEW GALLERIES TO GANDER AT

American Art
724 Central Ave., 501-624-0550
americanartgalleryandgifts.com

Artists' Workshop
601 A Central Ave., 501-623-6401
artistsworkshopgallery.com

Justus Fine Art
827 Central Ave. A, 501-321-2335
justusfineart.com

Whittington
307 Whittington Ave.

Art by the Park
338 Central Ave., 501-623-2363

Dryden Pottery
341 Whittington Ave., 501-623-4201
drydenpottery.com

CRAFT AND CELEBRATE
AT ARTS AND THE PARK

Arts and The Park is an annual 10-day spring festival showcasing the local arts scene. Produced by the Hot Springs Area Cultural Alliance, the festival takes place the last weekend in April, continuing through the first weekend in May, primarily throughout downtown Hot Springs. It includes everything from live performances to workshops, children's events, and art exhibitions. The idea of the festival is to promote Hot Springs as the art destination it has grown to be, and show the thousands of locals and visitors who attend what kind of art can be found in the Spa City year-round. There are different workshops and activities scheduled throughout the duration of the festival, and numerous local businesses participate, making it a collaborative communal effort in celebration of the arts.

501-321-2027
hotspringsarts.org

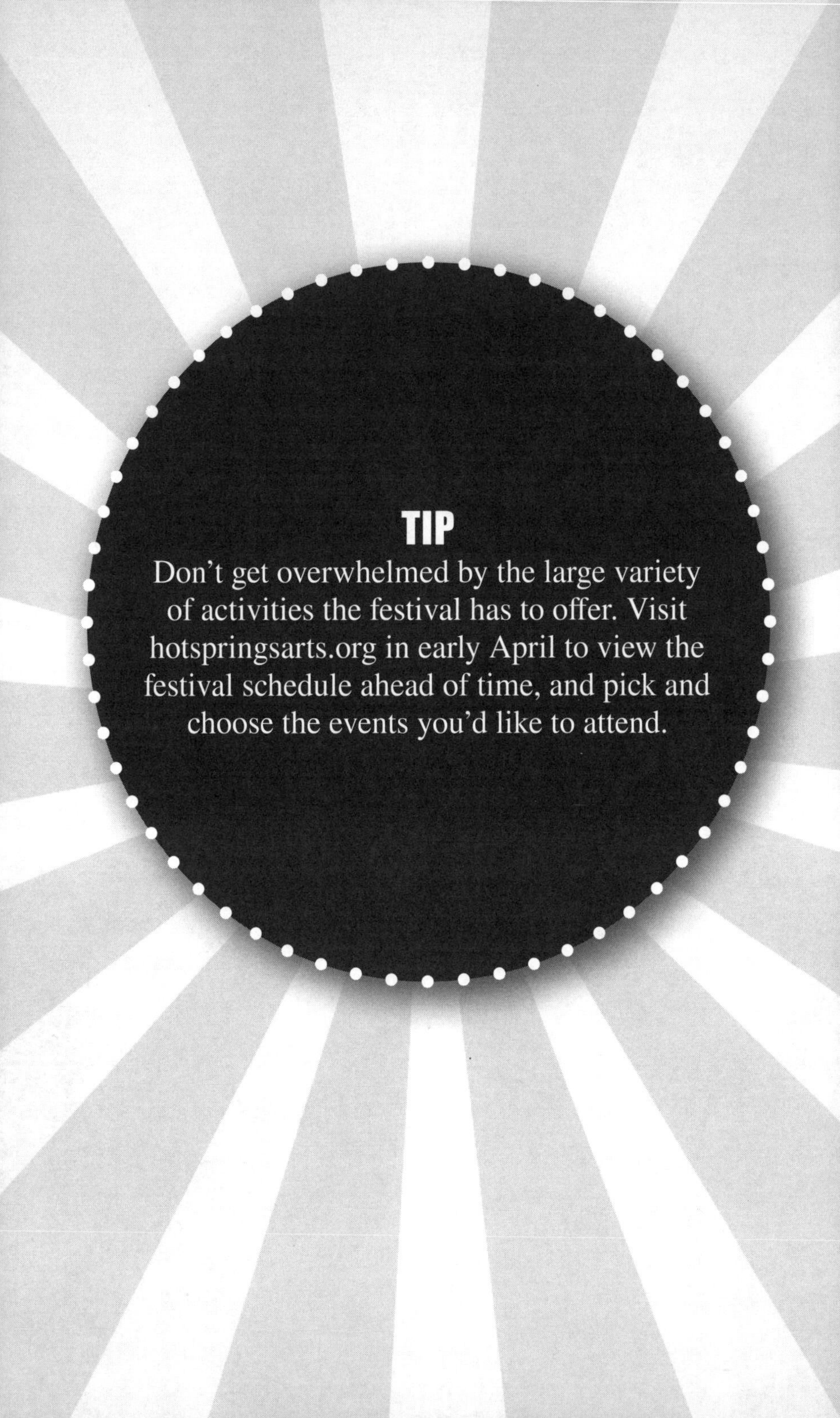
TIP
Don't get overwhelmed by the large variety of activities the festival has to offer. Visit hotspringsarts.org in early April to view the festival schedule ahead of time, and pick and choose the events you'd like to attend.

SHOPPING AND FASHION

BROWSE
THE FARMERS MARKET

The Hot Springs Farmers and Artisans Market is an Arkansas-only market, with the majority of vendors and farmers coming from Hot Springs and surrounding areas. There are a wide variety of 100% Arkansas-grown, -created, or -crafted items for sale at the market. From fresh produce and meat to handcrafted one-of-a-kind furniture pieces; from all-natural pet items to homemade body products; from inspiring original art to home-grown plants; and everything in between. The live music and friendly chatter creates a warm and inviting atmosphere as people browse. The Farmers Market has two seasons: main season and winter market. Main season operates from May to October, 7 a.m. to noon on Saturdays, and from June to August, 4 to 6 p.m. on Tuesdays. Winter market operates from November to April, 9 a.m. to noon on Saturday's.

121 Orange St., 501-262-8049
hotspringsfarmersmarket.com

TIP

The Farmers Market is seasonal. Collect information from your favorite vendors to see if they have a way for you to buy their products year-round.

86

SCRUB-A-DUB
AT THE BATHHOUSE SOAPERY AND CALDARIUM

Hot Springs National Park has drawn in the masses to be bathed in its thermal waters for decades, but the Bathhouse Soapery and Caldarium has that key ingredient needed for any good bath—the soap, of course! In this luxurious soapery located across from Bathhouse Row, you can find handcrafted bath and body products that are made, poured, and painted locally. But don't just take my word for the quality of the products. In this very hands-on environment customers are allowed, and encouraged, to do in-store touching, smelling, and trying of the products that pique their interest. The soapery also keeps up-to-date with seasonal fragrances, never leaving you lacking your beloved pumpkin spice, peppermint, or floral fragrances when the time comes.

366 Central Ave., 501-525-7627
bathhousesoap.com

87

PLAY DRESS UP
AT THE HOT SPRINGY DINGY

Need an extravagant costume for your next special event? Look to the Hot Springy Dingy for all your costume needs. In this brick and mortar shop you will find thousands of handmade, high-quality, one-of-a-kind costume pieces to choose from, allowing you to build your picture-perfect fit. And it's all for a phenomenal price, with the average costume rental running about $35. They have costumes from the biblical era and forward, as well as tuxedos, suits, and gowns of every variety. There are also numerous masks and plush heads to choose from. Complete any costume with the high-quality jewelry, makeup, and other accessories to choose from. Not finding just what you're looking for at the Hot Springy Dingy? The owners, who make all the costumes you'll see, take requests, ensuring that no one leaves without exactly what they set out for.

409 Park Ave., 501-623-2849

GET WITCHY
AT THE PARLOUR

Whether you're a seasoned sorceress or just fascinated by magic and spirits, this authentic occult shop will serve your every metaphysical need. As owner and operator Amy Davis always says: it's a place where spooky New England meets the primitive south. With an abundance of stones, tarot cards, pendulums, candles, educational books, herbs, incense, oddities and curios; Davis' stock is highly curated, as she conducts extensive research on all her products. The shop also offers professional tarot and palm readings, as well as custom-blended perfumes, oils, soaps, and incense by a witch at the shop's "Practical Witch Apothecary." Unique to the Hot Springs area, The Parlour is a one-stop shop allowing you to explore your spooky side and have a magical experience each visit.

340 Ouachita Ave., 501-701-4444
theparlourhs.com

SEIZE THE CLAY
AT DRYDEN POTTERY

A stop by Dryden Pottery, one of the last great American art pottery factories, is a must. Running since 1946, Dryden is a third generation-owned pottery shop that continues to throw new pottery weekly in-house with its custom-formulated glaze and clay. Each highly distinctive, one of a kind pottery piece is complete with a "Dryden" signature on the bottom. While you're browsing the sculptures, cups, bowls, plates and vases, be sure not to miss the star of the show: the "World's Tallest Wheel Thrown Vase." Like what you see? Sign up for a factory tour or potter's demonstration and allow Zack Dryden to mesmerize you with the "melody in glaze" he creates in mere moments using only clay and a spinning wheel.

341 Whittington Ave., 501-623-4201
drydenpottery.com

FIND YOUR ZEN
AT IT'S ALL ABOUT ROCKS

It's widely believed that stones have been impacting frequencies on the rock we live on since the inception of creation. The idea of the medicinal and healing energetic properties stones carry is not new, and continues to be popular. But where can you get stones that are thought to do so much? It's All About Rocks has you covered. At this metaphysical stone shop you can find hematite that works as an anti-inflammatory, shungite that grounds and protects you, or a tiger's eye that is thought to bring you simple luck. The list goes on and on with the hundreds of stones the shop offers. And if you're simply curious, come in and learn a bit more. Perhaps you'll leave with something that has the potential to change your life. Not into the stone magic? You may still leave with something from the shop's wide selection of Bohemian clothing, custom jewelry, or home decor.

350 Central Ave., 501-701-4356
itsaboutrocks.com

91

CELEBRATE THE MOST WONDERFUL TIME OF THE YEAR, ALL YEAR

AT KRINGLE'S

No matter what time of year you walk through the doors of Kringle's in the Park, the holiday spirit fills you, giving you that warm and fuzzy feeling typically only found on the morning of December 25th. From wall to wall, this year-round holiday store located in downtown Hot Springs is decorated with festive sparkles and glimmer. It's like stepping into Santa's headquarters. While there you will find holiday decor, collectables, ornaments, and gifts. And I haven't even gotten to the best part: across the street is the nostalgic holiday-themed sweet shop, Kringle's and Kones. The small section of downtown Kringle's inhabits gives you a taste, in more ways than one, of that wholesome holiday magic at any time.

118 B Central Ave., 501-762-0835

DISCOVER TOYS FROM YOUR CHILDHOOD
AT THE TOY CHEST

What ever happened to those Calico Critters or that Thomas the Train Engine that took up countless hours of your childhood? If you had your hands on whatever your favorite childhood toy or book was, I'm sure you'd like to pass the joy it brought you on to some other lucky kid out there. Well, you may just discover the long lost item at the Toy Chest. Since 1989 the Toy Chest has been providing both fun and learning to babies and children. From the classics to newer toys that foster development in growing tikes, the Chest is your one-stop shop for any child's gift. With many hands-on displays, the store is also just as fun for children to browse as it is for adults who may just find themselves in nostalgia heaven.

348 Central Ave., 501-623-4808
toychesthotsprings.com

THRIFT
THROUGH RETIRED LOCAL ARTICLES

It's hard to go wrong when thrifting in any city, but one way to go wrong when in Hot Springs is by not trying your hand at the craft at all. There are multiple thrift shops to sift through, and while even the generic Goodwill and Habitat for Humanity stores are worth visiting, there are some shops unique to just Hot Springs that have been known to have valuable treasures, from fine vintage clothing to antique furniture, hiding under dust. In a city full of fine people, you're bound to come across fine retired items, so sift diligently and you just may find some prized possessions at ludicrously low prices. And don't forget, it takes cleverness, savviness, and patience in order to be a successful thrifter. Now go forth and conquer.

TIP

Don't just take from the thrifts—donate, too! Especially during the wintertime, shops like Jackson House will hold items like donated coats to allow the homeless first picks.

THRIFTS TO CHOOSE FROM

Goodwill
631 E Grand Ave., 501-321-0275
205 Garrison Rd., 501-525-4473
goodwill.org

Re-Store
515 E Grand Ave., 501-321-4241
3825 AR-7, Hot Springs Village, 501-624-3333
garlandcountyhabitat.org

Jackson House
104 Jefferson St., 501-623-6641
jacksonhouse.org

Guardian Angels Cat Rescue Thrift
907 Hobson Ave., 501-623-3484
guardianangelscatshelter.org

Central Station Marketplace
3310 Central Ave., 501-623-4484

Thrift Stylin
1534 Malvern Ave., Ste. Y, 281-948-0233

Gently Worn
1623 Albert Pike Rd., 501-620-4048

Just Swanky
340 Ouachita Ave., 501-625-3003

TOP YOURSELF OFF
AT THE HOT SPRINGS HAT COMPANY

When in Hot Springs it's not hard to get swept away in the history of the gangsters or the fun of the Arkansas Derby, but be sure to do it right and dress the part. At the Hot Springs Hat Company, the largest hat store in Arkansas, there are plenty of hats for you to choose from. From Al Capone–style hats to extravagant feather hats traditionally worn at the Derby, you are sure to find something that suits that noggin. But the variety doesn't stop there; look to the Hat Company for your everyday, costume, or special-event hat, too. You can get a plain floppy hat, bucket hat, newsboy cap, top hat, fedora, or flat cap (just to name a few), and you always have the option to accessorize with the hat bands they have available.

332 Central Ave., 501-463-9210

ONE MORE PLACE FOR DERBY DAY HATS

Grand Lagniappe
811 W Grand Ave., 501-623-7799
grandlagniappe.com

EXPLORE THE EXTRAORDINARY
AT STELLA MAE'S

Stella Mae's is a subcultural celebration shop found in the heart of downtown that includes pinup, punk, and vintage styles. This sassy little shop has a wide selection of clothing, accessories, gifts, and homeware. So dive in and find something "out of the ordinary," like a Kit Cat Klock, vintage bathing suit, pair of fruit earrings, fashionable ascot, or Swami Oujia Talking Board. There's something for everyone, from a 12-year-old discovering different types of music through their band tees to a 60-year-old appreciating their beauty with one of Stella Mae's pinup-style dresses. Also, to make this feministic shop that much sweeter, much of its clothing comes from small, women-owned brands. So come one, come all—come to Stella Mae's because it's time to get funky.

410 Central Ave.
facebook.com/stellamaesretro

96

EXPERIENCE MEXICO
THROUGH THE DOORS OF LA BODEGUITA

La Bodeguita, translating to "little bodega," is the authentic Latin American supermarket sitting just off Central, dressed in blue and pink and serving as a hub for commerce and conversation. Despite its name, this little bodega is packed full of variety, culture, and services; from apartment and job listings to bank services to phone repairs, and that's just at the front counter. Walk through the grocery store and find an array of items produced in Mexico, including medicinal teas, over-the-counter medications, cleaning products, apparel, and piñatas. There are also local homemade products available, like special occasion cakes, breads, and ice cream bars. And don't forget to check out the produce section that has Latin American peppers, fruits, and herbs. But wait, there's more! In the back of this Bodega there is a dine-in restaurant serving a simple but authentic variety of affordable Latin American dishes.

1313 Central Ave., 501-620-4967

THREE MORE LOCAL MEXICAN GROCERS

La Bodeguita 2
510 Albert Pike Rd., 501-609-9580

Las Americas
114 Crawford St., 501-622-2544

La Potosina Meat Market
4737 Central Ave., 501-701-4856

GET TO KNOW THE LARKINS
AT FOX PASS

Even in a community full of remarkable artists, the work done by Jim and Barbara Larkin at Fox Pass stands out. These potters have been throwing, spinning, carving, building, and painting clay into incredible vases, pots, plates, and more since building their cozy little shop in 1973. Between Fox Pass and Dryden (previously mentioned), Hot Springs has been graced with two outstanding pottery establishments. The Larkins mix their own clay, resulting in durable stoneware in the final product that is chip-resistant and dishwasher and microwave safe. They also mix their glazes, resulting in unique and beautiful colors. Come to Fox Pass to watch the Larkin's at work, talk with them about their pottery journey, and perhaps pick up a piece or two from their showroom.

379 Fox Pass, 501-623-9906
foxpasspottery.com

DISCOVER THE NOVELTY
OF MIRACLE ELECTRONICS

Miracle Electronics is a hidden gem that you could miss if you happen to blink while passing by. And what would you be missing exactly? A collection of over 20,000 cassettes, CDs, 78s, 45s, and LPs. You could spend hours in this little shop that has been located in Hot Springs for over 30 years. The owner and operator, Darnell Weatherspoon, has albums (some new, but mostly used) in classical, rock and roll, rhythm and blues, hard rock, and country. There is likely not a genre he doesn't have, and many have scored records they have searched years for in this shop. But in addition to music, Weatherspoon also offers repairs on audio record players, as well as selling some equipment. If you're a fan of music, stop by Weatherspoon's.

203 A. Pleasant St., 501-538-6930

TIP

Virtually search through some of Weatherspoon's collection on disclogs.com, @miracleelect.

SHOP THE BOUTIQUES
OF THE SPA CITY

Beautiful garments line the racks of the boutiques scattered throughout the Spa City. Boutiques are kind of a different beast because the clothing is astounding, but the pricing tends to limit what you actually walk away with. So the only question is, which boutiques are the best to go to when looking to splurge on a few quality pieces for yourself? Lavish on Ouachita definitely makes the cut as one of the best, having items ranging from casual to prodigal, and a large range of prices. But don't stop there. Venture downtown and be sure to hit Joanna A., Snazzies, Faith & Flair, Red Sunflower, Bear Necessities and Jess & JoJo. And another one worth stopping by is the local staple Grand Lagniappe on Grand Avenue. Much thought is put in by these small boutique owners when carefully selecting the items they carry, so shoppers are in good hands.

Lavish
214 Ouachita Ave., 501-625-9515
lavishonmain.com

Joanna A.
800 Central Ave., 501-481-8106
joanna-a.com

Snazzies
258 Central Ave., 501-620-6005
shopsnazzies.com

Faith & Flair
126 Central Ave., 479-970-2489
faithandflair.com

Red Sunflower
404 Central Ave., 501-359-9647
facebook.com/shoptheredsunflowerboutique

Bear Necessities
422 Central Ave., 501-318-1225
facebook.com/theglitzygirlz

Jess & JoJo
412 Central Ave., Ste. A, 501-623-2672
facebook.com/shopjessandjojo

PERUSE
THE FRIENDS OF THE LIBRARY BOOK SALE

Browse hundreds of (mostly) gently used books, magazines, CDs, and DVDs at the Friends of the Library Book Sale in the Garland County Library. Pricing ranges anywhere from 10 cents to a few dollars, so go hunting and you might walk away with a treasure or two for an astounding price. Items sold come from community donations or retire from the library's circulation. Looking for more than just a mere fun read? You can also find resources like dictionaries, maps, and encyclopedias for cheap in the store. And the good news is that you don't have to be a library card holder to shop at the store—it's open to anyone!

1427 Malvern Ave., 501-623-4161
gclibrary.com

JUST ONE MORE BOOK STORE

Books-A-Million
450 Cornerstone Blvd., 501-525-1141
booksamillion.com

TIP

Friends of the Library is a nonprofit organization that works to raise funds for the Garland County Library, which is fine-free. Become a member to help financially support the local library and the book sale for $5 a year, or a lifetime fee of $100.

ACTIVITIES
BY SEASON

Hot Springs makes for a magical destination any time of year, but the weather and calendar can sometimes influence what should be a definite on your to-do list during certain times of the year. Here are some seasonal suggestions:

SPRING

SUMMER

Get Your Groove On at the Hot Springs Music Festival, 56

Swim at Lake Ouachita State Park, 72

Visit the Waterfall at Lake Catherine, 75

Take a Kahuna Bay Pontoon on Lake Hamilton, 84

Make a Splash at Magic Springs Theme and Water Park, 86

Browse the Farmers Market, 114

Tour the Biggest Tiny Town, 39

FALL

Watch Nine Days of Doc Films, 49

Embrace Your Fandom at Spa-Con, 54

Take a Scenic Drive through the Mountains, 43

Get a Better Look from the Mountain Tower, 61

Snag a Pretzel from the Biergarten of Steinhaus Keller, 10

Hike the Gulpha Gorge Trail, 77

Hear Local Ghost Stories on the Haunted Walking Tours, 100

See the Holiday Lights of the Chili Cook-Off, 52

Follow the Red Brick Road of the Grand Promenade, 76

Glow on the Row for Halloween, 55

WINTER

Drink a Cup of Locally Roasted Coffee at Red Light, 28

Explore the Ruins of the Abandoned Chewaukla Bottling Factory, 98

Browse the Farmers Market, 114

Celebrate the Most Wonderful Time of the Year, All Year at Kringle's, 120

Take a Horse-Drawn Carriage Ride, 106

SUGGESTED ITINERARIES

LAKE LIFE

ALL THINGS GANGSTER

FOR THE FAMILY

OUTDOOR EXPLORING

DATE NIGHT

Enjoy a Drink and a View from the Rooftop of The Waters, 21

Make a Splash at the Wine Bar, 26

Get Lucky at Oaklawn's Casino, 36

Blow Your Mind at a Maxwell Blade Magic Show, 40

Take a Horse-Drawn Carriage Ride, 106

Catch a Show at The Pocket Theatre, 44

Take Your Shoes off, Have a Roll, and Stay Awhile at Osaka, 20

Admire the Talent and Beauty of The Foul Play Cabaret, 46

Admire Local Art on a Gallery Walk, 108

Meet the Pirates of the Cove, 63

Make a Narrow Escape, 66

Blow Off Some Steam at Big Axe Battleground, 81

Attend the Longest Continuously Running Wednesday Night Poetry, 107

HERE FOR THE PARTY

Make a Splash at the Wine Bar, 26

Admire the Talent and Beauty of The Foul Play Cabaret, 46

Get Acquainted with Madam Maxine, 30

Celebrate Like the Irish at the World's Shortest St. Patrick's Day Parade, 50

Visit the Argentinian Bars, 32

Take a Sip from the Creek at Crystal Ridge Distillery, 12

Party on the Lake with Captain Jack, 45

Attend a Bridge Street Block Party, 53

Get Lucky at Oaklawn's Casino, 36

FOR THE FRUGAL

INDEX